HELPING SKILLS:
A BASIC TRAINING PROGRAM

by
Steven J. Danish
The Pennsylvania State University

and
Allen L. Hauer
The Ohio State University

ehavioral Publications   *New York*

Library of Congress Catalog Number 73-7834
Standard Book Number 87705-107-0
Copyright © 1973 by Behavioral Publications

BEHAVIORAL PUBLICATIONS
72 Fifth Avenue
New York, New York 10011

Printed in the United States of America

56789   987654

Library of Congress Cataloging in Publication Data

Danish, Steven J
    Helping skills.

    1. Paraprofessionals in social service--In-service
training--Handbooks, manuals, etc.   I. Hauer, Allen L.,
joint author.   I. Title.
HV11.D33   361'.007'15   73-7834
ISBN 0-87705-107-0

CONTENTS

ACKNOWLEDGEMENTS

It may sound trite to say that no book is the work of the authors alone. Yet, the development of this book has been influenced significantly by friends and colleagues whose contributions we wish to acknowledge.

Three individuals stand out. Norman Kagan, Allen Ivey, and Don MacLean have effected not only the direction of this book but have also influenced our growth as behavioral scientists. Don especially helped us develop the conceptual framework upon which the Program is based. Without his counsel this book would not have been written.

Many others, by the encouragement, support, suggestions and enthusiasm, have contributed to the Program. They include: Andy Horne, Tony Perino, Tony D'Augelli, Nancy Ferguson, Ed Vogelsong, Bob Graff, Pat Kipping, Herb Bolland, Hazel Scott, Dave Melby, Judy Braithwaite, and Cheryl Heisler. We respect their competence and acknowledge their help. In addition, feedback provided by students who were involved in the Counseling Adjunct Program; namely, Mike Damian, Beverly Zaremba, Leanne Waiau, Jim Rouse, Rick Merabile and Herb Stockley was invaluable. Also, we are grateful to Richard Rasche for his permission to use the helpee-simulated statements in Stage III.

We owe a special debt of gratitude to Clay Ladd who as director of the Counseling Center at Southern Illinois University provided an atmosphere where pursuing our own interests was encouraged. Furthermore, Mary Jane Adcock and Sheron L. Sefchick, our typists, deserve special thanks for suffering through the numerous revisions of the Program.

Finally, we wish to thank our families, Carole, Kyle and Christopher Danish and Janet Hauer for their support and caring. We dedicate this book to them in the hope that we too can learn from this Program and become increasingly more sensitive members of our families.

S. J.D.
A. L. H.

INTRODUCTION

The objective of this experience is to assist you in becoming a more effective helper. The Program emphasizes three basic components involved in being a helper: 1) an understanding of yourself; 2) some knowledge of helping skills and 3) experience in applying these skills. Obviously, one never knows all there is to know about himself or about the techniques used to help others. This is especially true if the learning is to be done in a specified time period. Since the time period for this experience is short, it is important to realize the limitation on your learning. At the conclusion of the *Helping Skills: A Basic Training Program,* you cannot expect to have a complete repertoire of helping strategies. However, you will know more about yourself and about how to be helpful to others.

I. THE PROCESS OF TRAINING

Research studies have found that learning is facilitated when the procedure of training to be used is made as explicit as possible. There is no mystical or magical process involved in learning to be a helper. The intention of this Introduction is to make the goals and processes of training as clear as possible. It is expected that when you have questions about what the trainer(s) is doing or why, you will ask them. Part of the effectiveness of the teaching-learning process is being committed to what you are learning. If you are aware of what you are doing, your learning will be facilitated.

Below is the format to be used to assist you in learning the skills involved in being an effective helper. This procedure is detailed in order that you may become acquainted with what you will be learning and how you will be learning it:

1. Identify and define the skill to be learned.
2. Discuss the need for learning the skill.
3. Specify the level of skill attainment necessary to demonstrate that the skill is understood. An attainment level is specified so that both you and the trainer are aware of how effective you are in utilizing the skill. In this way, you can practice until you reach the prescribed level. Also, you have a record of what you can and cannot do.
4. Observe models demonstrating both effective (high skill levels) and ineffective (low skill levels) examples.
5. Practice the skill to the point that you can demonstrate that the skill has been learned.
6. Become acquainted with the next skill.

II. AN OUTLINE OF THE PROGRAM

There are six separate stages, all of which attempt to integrate the three basic components necessary for effective helping: an understanding of yourself, some knowledge of helping skills, and experience in applying these skills. The six stages are:

Stage   I.   Understanding Your Needs to be a Helper
Stage II.   Using Effective Nonverbal Behavior
Stage III.   Using Effective Verbal Behavior
Stage IV.   Using Effective Self Involving Behavior
Stage V.   Understanding Others' Communication
Stage VI.   Establishing Effective Helping Relationships.

As you can see the purpose is threefold. Two of the stages emphasize self learning (I and IV), two emphasize skill learning (II and III), and two emphasize the application of these skills (V and VI). All the stages involve some learning in each component; for example, all stages provide practice in applying what you learn.

The program is based on "the block building principle." In other words, each successive stage is based on and requires successful completion of the previous stage. If you do not understand a section or cannot complete it, ask for assistance before going on.

STAGE I. UNDERSTANDING YOUR NEEDS TO BE A HELPER

GOAL

To become aware of one's need for being a helper.

RATIONALE

The first goal is a skill which upon achievement should provide you with an increased understanding of yourself and, in turn, should facilitate your becoming an effective helper.

Two common responses that are given by future people-helpers when asked why they wish to become helpers are:

1. I never met a person I didn't like.
2. I love the world and want to help everyone.

One should be suspicious of these responses. That is not to say that people who make such statements are not to be believed. However, they may not be totally aware of their motivation for helping. One can be helpful to people in a number of ways, some of which are more direct than being a people-helper. For example, our society needs sanitation workers (garbage men) and nurses' aides. Why not help people by functioning in one of these positions?

In addition, many people in whom others confide are individuals who appear to have no problems of their own. Although some people may not have problems, most do. These individuals may not feel secure enough to discuss their problems with others. Because of their own insecurity they encourage the confidences of others.

This discussion is not an attempt to discourage your desire to be a people-helper nor to make light of your past attempts to help others. However, you should be sensitive to your motivations for helping. Who you are and why you want to help people influences what happens in a helping relationship. For example, if a helper has a need to be needed and depended upon, he might extend a helping relationship too long in order to gratify these needs.

ATTAINMENT LEVEL

To discuss your motivation for being a people-helper as honestly as possible.

PROCEDURE

1. As a group, discuss the implications of talking about oneself, for example, what kind of reaction do you have to talking about yourself?

2. Discuss in dyads your reasons for wanting to become a helper.

3. Examine your conversation. Was it characterized by a discussion of: a) who you are and what you do ("name, rank and serial number"), b) past experiences and events which influenced your decision to become a helper, or c) your present needs and motivations for helping?

4. Observe models, either live or on film, who discuss their needs to be helpers and use low skill levels.

5. Using low skill methods, discuss why you wish to become a helper in the same dyads.

6. Observe models who discuss their needs to be helpers using high skill levels. Following the discussion one model will summarize his understanding of what his partner's needs and motivations for helping are. The partner will then provide feedback on the accuracy of the summary. The process will be repeated until the summarizer can identify clearly his partner's needs and motives. The two models will then reverse roles.

7. Using high skill levels, discuss your reasons for wanting to be a helper in the same dyads. Focus on why you want to help people and what needs of yours are met by being a helper. Following the discussion, repeat the process demonstrated by the models.

(Listening to another's comments about being a helper, and then summarizing those comments is of value not only in identifying one's own needs and motivations, but also as an exercise in learning how to listen, a skill which will be focused on later. By indicating your own feelings about being a people-helper, and by having another person summarize your statements, you should be aided in learning how to speak clearly and how to make yourself understood.)

8. Compare your first conversation (Step 2) with this last interaction (Step 7). Did they differ and if so, how? Then return to the large group and discuss what differences occurred, if any, as a total group.

9. Homework:
   a. Read over Stage I especially the evaluation of the attainment level.
   b. Read the material written by others on their needs to help (pages 13-14).
   c. Meet with another group member and repeat Step 7.
   d. Meet with someone you know well who is not in the group and discuss with him your needs and motivations for helping.
   e. Write a description of your needs and motivation to be a helper (to be handed in).
   f. Read Stage II which will be dealt with in the second session.

EVALUATION OF ATTAINMENT LEVEL

At the second session you will be asked to repeat Step 7 with a third group member. There are two criteria involved in the attainment level: (1) your own understanding of your needs to be a helper, and (2) your ability to communicate clearly these needs to another. Two sources of evaluation will be employed to assess your attainment level for both criteria: (1) your own perceptions of how well you understand your needs and communicate them to others, and (2) your partner's perception of how well you understand your needs and communicate them to him. A *Behavioral Checklist* is included on page 7 to aid in this evaluation. The purpose of the Checklist in this stage and future stages is to give some indication of how well you are achieving the skill being evaluated. A number of components of the skill are broken down so that you may assess your progress and deficiencies.

If your self perception and your partner's perception of you are fairly consistent, the evaluation is likely to be accurate. If there is a significant discrepancy between your self evaluation and your partner's evaluation of you consult the trainer or attempt the evaluation again with another partner.

It should be noted that the two criteria are relatively independent. It is possible for an individual to understand his needs but not be able to effectively communicate them. A perceptive listener may be able to understand this. In addition, an individual may clearly communicate some of his felt needs but the listener may perceive that he does not have a clear understanding of his real needs. Therefore, although the two criteria may seem similar at times, they are not.

If your evaluation indicates a high level of skill, you can feel comfortable progressing to Stage II, although it is reasonable to assume that as you become more involved in people-helping, your motivation may change or your understanding of your needs may increase. Either way, it is helpful to keep this stage in mind.

If your evaluation indicates a less than high level of skill, one of two things may be happening. Either you have difficulty expressing yourself or you are unclear about what your motivations are. In both instances, it is important that you raise your skill level before going further. If you are having difficulty, consult the trainer.

QUESTIONS FOR THOUGHT

The following are some questions for you to consider both as you evaluate yourself on Stage I and as you advance through the program. At this point: 1) Do you feel as if your needs are strong enough for you to commit yourself to the process of learning to be a helper? If so, why? 2) Do you feel that your needs can be fulfilled by helping others? If so, why?

BEHAVIORAL CHECKLIST I
UNDERSTANDING YOUR NEEDS TO BE A HELPER

NAME _____

PARTNER _____

	Partner's Evaluation		*Your own Evaluation*	
	Yes	No	Yes	No
A. Was your conversation characterized:				
1. By a discussion of who you are and what you do ("name, rank, and serial number")?	___	___	___	___
2. By a discussion of past experiences and events which influenced your decision to become a helper ("Ever since I had Mrs. Jones in 3rd grade I've always wanted to be a teacher")?	___	___	___	___
3. By a discussion focusing on your present needs and motivations for helping?	___	___	___	___
B. Was your partner able to summarize accurately your needs to be a helper the first time?	___	___	___	___
C. Have you achieved a sufficiently high level of skill to progress to Stage II?	___	___	___	___

TO BE HANDED IN

Stage I

EVALUATION OF ATTAINMENT LEVEL REPORT

NAME _____

PARTNER _____

1. To what degree do you understand your needs to be a helper?

TO BE HANDED IN

2. (For your partner to complete.) On the basis of what you know of your partner, to what degree do you think he understands his needs to be a helper?

3. To what degree do you think you communicate clearly your needs to be a helper?

4. (For your partner to complete.) On the basis of what you know about your partner, do you think he communicates clearly his needs to be a helper?

5. If your skill level is less than either you would like it to be or your partner thinks it should be, outline a specific plan for increasing the skill level.

SAMPLES OF HOMEWORK ASSIGNED IN STAGE I

1. What My Needs and Motivations Are For Helping People

Rather than being an easy task, I think it is very difficult for a person like me to disclose what personal needs are met by helping someone. People who make great big generalizations about how they "like people" and "like to feel needed" are easy people to "read."

I think they have bigger egos and greater self-interest. When I find myself in a helping position I think I am generally more concerned about the individual in front of me.

In no way am I a welcome mat for the whole world's problems. I don't take on unnecessary burdens such as offering to take care of other peoples' children or pets nor listen to all their problems. I have no need whatsoever to have the "public" in general see me as noble and self-sacrificing.

When I have helped a person, many times I was aware that my behavior was as "warming" or "comforting" to me as the "other" found it to be. For example, I know when I meet strangers I try to make them feel welcome and comfortable. I find this quite easy to do, whereas others seem shyer under these circumstances. Although I can certainly be called shy and not confident in other situations, I seem able to project a warmth that is helpful to others in this situation. I know that this knack gives me pleasure. It may be simply that I enjoy knowing that finally I am better at something than my associates are.

Again, in a personal setting, when I am helpful I think it may relate to my enjoyment of being known as a warm, caring person rather than a self-centered, cold individual.

When I have been helpful professionally, my only satisfaction is in realizing that in a one-to-one relationship my concern does show. I think I can have some power in shaping the involvement or relationship. If you are helping you are obviously in control. This is very awesome and pleasant for someone who is fairly passive and not pushy or who generally lacks the self-confidence to be a leader in other types of relationships.

Finally, sometimes when I have been helpful it has helped me overlook some of my own problems. It helps to get so involved in others that I forget about myself.

2. What My Needs and Motivations Are For Helping People

Why do I want to help people? Well, that's easy enough: helping is good, true, virtuous, beautiful, American, Christian, and just about any other positive adjective I can think of. Honestly, though, I guess I need to—it makes me feel good and feel wanted.

I like people saying things such as "you're a real friend, always there when I need you," or "you're so good, always willing to help."

Also, I have to admit that helping does make me feel a little superior. I don't think that it's so bad; it's mostly the truth. I mean, you don't often help someone if he's better at it than you are. I think that people have to feel superior sometimes. I remember back in high school a group of us used to tutor orphan children after school and have holiday parties for them. We had so much fun helping those children. It really was nice knowing that you had more intelligence, love at home, and money, and could share it with others.

When I was young I would get into self-pitying moods (as I still do occasionally). At those times my mother would insist that I look at and talk to others less fortunate than I was. Corny sounding, huh? But, you know, it works! The more time I spend listening to other people's troubles, the better my life seems to be in comparison.

Basically, I really want people to like me. Although quite a common sentiment, everyone uses different means to accomplish this goal. One of the easiest ways for me to get people to like me is to help them.

Deep down, in the most unpleasant part of me, I sense that I do want people to feel indebted to me when I help them. I want them to be there when I need help, to trade love and friendship for help, and to be grateful. Sometimes I feel I'm getting more than I'm giving under the guise of helping someone else.

I guess if I look at my most base motivation, I would have to say I like the potential control over another: the knowledge that you can greatly influence another person's life. When you are helping, you are the more knowledgeable one, the leader, and the helpee will often follow your suggestions.

As I think about what I've written, I really don't like myself very much. I wonder if others feel this way. I like people and want to help and it scares me to understand what my reasons really are.

STAGE II. USING EFFECTIVE NONVERBAL BEHAVIOR

GOAL

To exhibit good non-verbal attending behavior in interpersonal situations.

RATIONALE

Good attention is a necessary component for good communication. Researchers are becoming increasingly aware of the effect of persuasion and expertness as factors in helping others. It is said by some that when a helper appears to be competent and shows that he believes in what he does, the helpee *feels* more comfortable and is more likely to trust the help or advice given to him. For example, most of you are probably acquainted with the use of placebos (sugar pills) that physicians sometimes give to cure imaginary illnesses some patients have.

However, it is important to understand that merely portraying a competent person does not make one so and that the people you meet will have real problems. The purpose of teaching you good attentive skills is not to enable you to put something over on someone. (We have all been exposed to the slick, persuasive salesman who wants to sell you ice in the winter). The purpose of this stage is to aid you in making the most of your ability by assisting you in the development of the skills necessary in helping others.

DEFINITIONS

1. Eye Contact

Good eye contact consists of looking at another individual when he is talking to you or when you are talking to him. Eye contact should be spontaneous glances which express an interest and desire to communicate.

Poor eye contact consists of never looking at another individual; staring at him constantly and blankly; and looking away from him as soon as he looks at you.

2. Postural position (including gestural and facial expressions)

Good postural position includes: sitting with one's body facing another person; hands either on lap or desk loosely clasped or *occasionally* being used to gesturally in-

15

dicate what is being communicated verbally; being responsive facially, i.e., spontaneous smiling or nodding of head in agreement or understanding and frowning when
not understanding; an erect but not rigid body and an occasional leaning toward
the other to emphasize a verbal point being made or to indicate a "withness" to the
other.

Poor postural position includes: sitting with body and head not facing another person; slouching; sitting in a very fixed, rigid position without moving; being restless or
fidgety; being preoccupied with hands, papers on lap or desk; cleaning fingernails;
making no gestures at all with hands; constant movement and thrashing of hands
and arms; no facial expression (stonefaced); too much inappropriate smiling, frowning
or nodding of head.

3. Verbal quality

Good verbal quality includes: a pleasant, interested intonation; speech neither too
loud nor too soft; reflection of the affect appropriate to the message being communicated; a choice of words which facilitates the listener's understanding of the communication.

Poor verbal quality includes: a flat, dull tone of voice; irrelevant and/or uninterested
responses; a quivering voice; speech either too loud or too soft; excessive use of jargon
or "psychologese"; the excessive use of such filler words as "you know."

ATTAINMENT LEVEL

1. To be able to identify and discriminate the components of good and poor attending behavior.

2. To be able to use good attending behavior.

PROCEDURE

1. Meet in small groups of 4-6 to express emotional concepts non-verbally. The
trainer will assign an emotion for each member of the small group to express non-verbally. (A partial list of emotions is: hate, despair, trust, love, joy, anxiety, uncertainty,
frustration, embarrassment, anger, disinterest and hostility.) You are to express your
assigned emotion by using gestures and other non-verbal communications. You are
also allowed to recite the alphabet and through your voice and the manner with which
you recite the alphabet express this emotion. The important thing is to express yourself without using words. The other members of your small group are to guess what
the non-verbally expressed emotion is.

2. As a total group consider the definitional components of good and poor attending behavior and their implications in the helping relationship.

3. Meet in dyads and discuss any topic you wish. How effective is your attending behavior?

4. Observe models either live or on film, using poor attending behavior.

5. Meet in the same dyads and discuss any topic you wish while using poor attending behavior.

6. Identify each other's poor attending behavior. Following this, return to the large group and discuss your reactions to an interaction with an individual using poor attending behavior.

7. Observe models demonstrating good attention behavior.

8. Meet in triads. One individual should take the role of discussant, the second the listener and the third the observer. The discussant should converse with the listener on any topic he wishes. Following the interaction, the observer and listener should provide feedback to the discussant on his attending behavior and the observer and discussant provide feedback to the listener on his attending behavior. Each individual should have an opportunity to play each role.

9. Homework:

    a. Reread Stage II especially the section on "evaluation of attainment level."

    b. Observe the good and poor attending behavior of others.

    c. Observe the non-verbal attending and communication behavior of three dyads in conversation. Complete a *Behavioral Checklist* on each dyad. After you have completed the Checklist, write up your impressions about: (1) what you think the two are talking about, (2) how interested were the members of the dyad in the conversation, (3) what attitudes and feelings were being conveyed non-verbally(i.e., trust, love, joy, contempt, frustration, anxiety, etc.)? What *specific* non-verbal cues led to your impression about the above three questions? The questions as well as the *Behavioral Checklist* are to be handed in.

    d. Practice communicating with others non-verbally during the week.

    e. Practice good attending behavior with others with whom you interact during the week.

    f. If an audiotape recorder is available, meet with another individual, record a conversation and be sure to focus on your verbal quality.

    g. Teach good attending behavior to a friend during the week.

    h. Read Stage III to be dealt with in the third session.

    i. Complete questions 1 and 2, Part A, of The Evaluation of Attainment Level Report, Stage II before the next session.

EVALUATION OF ATTAINMENT LEVEL

At the third session, new triads will be formed and Step #8 will be repeated with the inclusion of *Behavioral Checklist II.*

The feedback provided by the observer and listener when you are the discussant and by the observer and discussant when you are the listener will serve as one source of evaluation. Your own subjective assessment of your non-verbal attending behavior will serve as a second source. If the two sources are fairly consistent, the evaluation is likely to be accurate. If there is a significant discrepancy between your self evaluation and the evaluation of the other triad members, attempt the evaluation again with two other individuals in the group. The trainer will be willing to act as the observer.

If your evaluation indicates a high level of attending behavior, you can feel comfortable progressing to Stage III. However, it is essential that you continually practice good attending behavior so that it becomes an integral part of your interactions with others. If your evaluation indicates less than a high level of attending behavior, you should first identify the areas you need to improve and then practice them with another group member. To work with someone who has a good facility with non-verbal attending behavior might be helpful, since you will be provided with a good model.

BEHAVIOR CHECKLIST II
NON-VERBAL ATTENDING BEHAVIOR

TRIAD MEMBERS _____

_____

_____

Behavior Observed (Check if observed)

	You as a Discussant		You as a Listener	
	Ob-server	Listener	Ob-server	Dis-cussant
A. Face and Head Movements				
1. Uses affirmative head nods	——	——	——	——
2. Face rigid	——	——	——	——
3. Calm, yet expressive use of facial movements	——	——	——	——
4. Blankly staring	——	——	——	——
5. Turning eyes away when another looks at him (her)	——	——	——	——
6. Spontaneous eye movements and eye contact	——	——	——	——
7. Not looking at other when talking	——	——	——	——
8. Looks directly at other person when he (she) talks	——	——	——	——
9. Extraneous facial movements	——	——	——	——
B. Hand and Arm Movements				
10. Spontaneous and fluid use of hand and arms	——	——	——	——
11. No gesturing (arms rigid)	——	——	——	——
12. Makes physical contact with other person (shakes hands, touches arm, etc.)	——	——	——	——
13. Uses hand movements for emphasis	——	——	——	——
14. Inappropriate arm and hand movements	——	——	——	——

	You as a Discussant		You as a Listener	
	Ob-server	Listener	Ob-server	Dis-cussant
C. Body Movements				
15. Slouching	____	____	____	____
16. Relaxed posture but not slouching	____	____	____	____
17. Sitting in fixed, rigid position	____	____	____	____
D. Body Orientation				
18. Body positioned toward other	____	____	____	____
19. Physically distant from person	____	____	____	____
20. Sits close to person with whom talking	____	____	____	____
21. Not facing other with body	____	____	____	____
E. Verbal Quality				
22. Voice quiver	____	____	____	____
23. Speech blocks or stammers	____	____	____	____
24. Lack of affect	____	____	____	____
25. Inappropriate affect	____	____	____	____
26. Too loud	____	____	____	____
27. Too soft	____	____	____	____
28. Excessive use of jargon	____	____	____	____
29. Excessive use of "psychologese"	____	____	____	____
30. Excessive use of "you know"	____	____	____	____
31. Too fast	____	____	____	____
32. Too slow	____	____	____	____
F. Have you achieved a sufficiently high level of skill to progress to Stage III?	____	____	____	____

Stage II

EVALUATION OF ATTAINMENT LEVEL REPORT

NAME _____

PARTNERS _____

A. The first two questions are based on your behavior during Procedure #1 and should be completed prior to the Stage III Meeting.

1. What emotions or attitudes do you seem to have difficulty expressing? Why are these difficult and how can you overcome these deficiencies? Which ones are easy for you to express?

2. Which emotions or attitudes do you have difficulty identifying when expressed by someone else? Why are these difficult and how can you overcome these deficiencies? Which ones are easy for you to identify?

B. The remaining questions pertain to your behavior during the evaluation of attainment level exercise to be done at the beginning of the third session. These should be completed immediately following the evaluation.

1. From your perception, what effective non-verbal attending behavior do you have difficulty expressing?

2. From the perceptions of the observer and receiver, what effective non-verbal attending behaviors do you have difficulty expressing?

3. Describe specifically your plans for improving your ineffective non-verbal attending behavior(s).

STAGE III. USING EFFECTIVE VERBAL BEHAVIOR

GOAL

To exhibit effective verbal response behavior in interpersonal situations. Effective verbal response is the ability to accurately distinguish and use different categories of response. There are two major response types: continuing and leading. These terms will be defined and explained in detail in this section.

RATIONALE

Just as good non-verbal attending behavior is a necessary component for good communication, so is effective verbal behavior. Without effective verbal communication it is extremely difficult to establish a meaningful relationship with another and this characteristic is essential to helping others. No one will accept your help if he doesn't trust or relate to you. If you can't communicate with him, your relationship will be poor. You must make him aware that you want to understand and help him and that you are a person who can be helpful. This is not an easy task. People have impressions quickly and judge the person with whom they are communicating. What you say and how you say it will play an important part in establishing a relationship.

PART A—RESPONSE TYPES

CONTINUING RESPONSES

Continuing responses generally serve two purposes. The first is as a reinforcer for a person to continue talking. Your verbal behavior like your non-verbal behavior can be reinforcing or non-reinforcing. Non-verbally, if you want someone to continue talking you may smile or nod your head in agreement or understanding. If you want to stop a conversation you may frown or look puzzled. Equally as effective in communicating your understanding is a continuing verbal response. Failure to respond verbally may make a helpee confused and unable to discern whether you understand him or care about his problem. He will probably stop talking or change the subject.

The second purpose is to help the helpee clarify what he is saying and to provide him with an understanding of his problems by helping him hear what he is saying to himself. Below are definitions of three continuing responses. While they are important ones, they are by no means the only ones.

DEFINITIONS

1. "Mm Hm"

This response is the most simple verbal response. It communicates "withness": "Continue, I'm listening and I understand."

2. Content Response

This response is an attempt to help both you and the helpee understand what the helpee has been saying. The focus of this response is to echo or mirror the *content* of what the helpee has said.
   Example:

Helpee: I am not sure what to do. If I stay at school I will need to make up two courses plus take two new courses and find a job. If I go home to the junior college I could make up the two courses at night and work for my father during the day.

Helper: Let me see if I understand the problem (Let me try and summarize (clarify) what I hear the problem to be). You're not sure whether to stay here and be a full-time student or go home and attend the junior college at night and work for your father. Is that accurate?

3. Affective Response

This response is difficult to achieve because one must be aware of the content of the response as well as the *feelings or affect within* the response. In other words, you must reach into the content and pull out the *feelings*. Therefore, you should be listening carefully to the helpee and be aware not only of what he says *but how he says it!* You must try to understand how the helpee feels and respond to his feelings. Since you are responding to his feelings rather than his words, sometimes it is best to be tentative in your responses. For example, you might preface your response by saying:
   It seems to me you're saying . . .
   Perhaps you feel . . .
   It sounds like . . .
   Are you saying . . .
   Examples:

Helpee: It's hard to get a date. I've been out of touch with the other girls since I was dating Ann.

Helper: It sounds to me as if you're afraid to try to get another date; afraid of being hurt again.

Helpee: (laughingly) I'm really upset about my grades this quarter; I'm not sure what I'll do if I flunk out.

Helper: School seems to be a joke to you this quarter. It seems to me that you couldn't care less about it.

GUIDELINES FOR MAKING EFFECTIVE CONTINUING RESPONSES

1. Content

The first step in learning to give content responses is to be able to repeat or "mirror" what the other individual has said using tentative introductory phrases such as "Are you saying . . ." or "It seems to me that you're . . ." For example:

Helpee: Sometimes she really seems to like me and then all of a sudden, she gets angry at me.

Helper: Are you saying that sometimes she seems to like you but then all of a sudden, she gets angry at you?

You should practice making "mirror" responses until you are able to do so with ease.

Obviously, if a helper did nothing but make mirror responses, the helpee would soon get angry or bored. Therefore, you need to develop a higher level of skill in making content responses. This higher level of skill is exemplified by a helper who can respond to the helpee's statement in a manner which is *concise and in the helper's own words*. For example:

Helpee: Sometimes she really seems to like me and then all of a sudden she gets angry at me.

Helper: Her behavior is inconsistent toward you.

You should practice these "concise, own words" responses until you feel at ease with them.

2. Affective

These responses are perhaps the most difficult to learn because feelings and emotions are often difficult to identify in others. Earlier, some guidelines were given to help you distinguish feelings from thoughts. What is presented now are some of the steps involved in learning to make skillful affective responses.

First, you should identify the feeling being expressed. Non-verbal behaviors and voice quality are often cues to this identification process. Many times your identification will be based more on intuition than any clear reasoning. This is appropriate. It is important to use your intuition or your best guess about what feelings are being expressed. Often, these vague hunches have validity. If you are unable to identify the feeling by intuition, try to place yourself in the situation and express how you would feel under the same circumstances. While one must be aware that individuals feel and react differently to similar circumstances, you may get some notion of the feelings the other person is expressing. Thus, while in the initial learning process of expressing affective responses, you should focus on identifying the emotion being expressed, e.g., anger, love, hate, etc., and get feedback on the accuracy of your perception. When you are able to identify accurately the feelings being expressed, the second step is to translate the identification of feelings into sentences. It is useful to start such sentences with a tentative introduction: for example, "It sounds like you're feeling . . ." In addition, try to gauge your reaction to the same level of the feeling being expressed. For example:

Helpee: (Angrily) I'm not sure how I feel!
Helper: It sounds to me as if you're damn mad!

ATTAINMENT LEVEL

1. Be able to identify the different continuing responses.
2. Be able to use the different continuing responses.
3. As a part of learning to use affective responses, be able to recognize the general feeling states of others.

PROCEDURE

1. As a group, discuss the definitions and uses of continuing responses.
2. As a group, listen to a series of helper-helpee interactions, either live or recorded, and identify the helper's continuing responses.
  ✓ 3. In triads, listen to a series of helpee statements. Write down different content responses to the statements. With the assistance of the others in the triad, each member of the triad should determine whether he was able to make effective content responses. Each trainee should make "mirror" responses until the other members of the triad feel that he is adequately skilled at this kind of response. Then, each trainee should repeat the same process using "concise, own words" responses.
4. Meet in the same triads and use content responses in a modified role playing situation. One individual should take the role of the "helper," a second the "helpee," and the third the observer. Following the modified role playing situation, the observer and "helpee" should provide feedback about the "helper's" content responses. As in Step 3, each trainee should become proficient at "mirror" responses before using "concise, own words" responses. Each member of the triad should play each role. On page 41 there are a series of helpee simulated statements that may be used if the triad desires.
5. In different triads, listen to a series of helpee statements. Write down different affective responses to the statements. With the assistance of the others in the triad, each member of the triad should determine whether he was able to make effective responses. Each trainee should first practice identifying the "helpee's" feelings until other members of the triad feel that he is proficient at this process. Then, each trainee should repeat the procedure using "complete-sentence affective" responses.

6. Meet in the same triads and use affective responses in a modified role playing situation. One individual should take the role of the "helper," a second the "helpee," and the third the observer. Following the modified role playing situation, the observer and "helpee" should provide feedback about the "helper's" affective responses. As in Step 5, the "helper" should become proficient in identifying the feelings before translating them into "complete sentence affective" responses. Each member of the triad should play each role. On page 41 there are a series of response leads that may be used if the triad desires.

7. Homework:
   a. Reread the definitions of the different continuing responses so that you are clear on the distinctions.
   b. Practice using the various continuing responses with another group member. Use the modified role playing statements as a guide if necessary.
   c. Respond, in writing, to be handed in, to several modified role playing statements using the various continuing responses. Respond to statements 21-25 using content responses and 26-30 using affective responses (page 41).
   d. Practice the responses in your daily interactions with others. Which type of response do you use most often?
   e. Read the section on *Leading Responses* for the next session.

EVALUATION OF ATTAINMENT LEVEL

Two evaluation procedures will be used:

1. Listen to models and identify their various continuing responses. You should be able to identify correctly the majority of the responses. If you are not able to identify correctly the various continuing responses, you will not be able to use them effectively.

2. In triads, each individual will be asked to respond to another by using all the continuing responses in a modified role playing situation. *Behavioral Checklist III—Part A* is to be used as a guideline. One member of the triad should take the role of "helper," the second the "helpee," and the third the observer. Each individual should have an opportunity to play each role. Feedback will be provided by the observer and "helpee" on the "helper's" facility with the different continuing responses. The feedback will serve as one source of evaluation. Your own subjective assessment will serve as a second source. If the two sources are fairly consistent, the evaluation is likely to be accurate. If there is significant discrepancy between your self evaluation and the evaluation of the observer and "helpee," attempt the evaluation again with another observer and "helpee". The trainer will be willing to act as the observer.

If your evaluation indicates a high level of continuing verbal response behavior, you can feel comfortable progressing to the section on *Leading Responses*. However, it is essential that you continually practice these responses so that they become an integral part of your interactions with others. If your evaluation indicates a less than high level, you should first identify the responses you need to improve upon and then practice them with another group member. Working with someone who exhibits a good facility with the responses you need to practice might be helpful as he will provide you with a good model.

BEHAVIORAL CHECKLIST III (PART A)
CONTINUING RESPONSE BEHAVIOR

	Yes	No
A. Are you able to identify correctly the following responses?		
1. Content	___	___
2. Affective	___	___

	Observer's Evaluation		"Helpee's" Evaluation		You own Evaluation	
	Yes	No	Yes	No	Yes	No
B. Are you able to use accurately the following responses?						
1. Content						
a. "Mirror"	___	___	___	___	___	___
b. "concise, own words"	___	___	___	___	___	___
2. Affective						
a. identification of feelings	___	___	___	___	___	___
b. "complete-sentence affective"	___	___	___	___	___	___
c. Have you achieved a sufficiently high level of skill to progress to the next section?	___	___	___	___	___	___

LEADING RESPONSES

Leading responses change the nature of the helping relationship. When continuing responses are used, the responsibility for the direction of discussion rests with the helpee. The helper acts as a sounding board or mirror. Leading responses put more responsibility for change on the helper. The helper communicates non-verbally the following: "If you listen to me and do what I say, we can work out this problem." The goal of these responses is mainly behavior change, and to a lesser degree, understanding.

The helper must be careful when leading responses are used. He must have listened sufficiently to the helpee so that his leads are not premature; so that he understands the problem and *can* be helpful. *Often, helpers will use leading responses before adequately understanding the helpee's concern and gaining his trust.* However, when the helper feels he does understand the problem and that leading will be helpful, he should do so.

1. Influencing

An influencing response is used to change the attitudes, beliefs or behavior of the helpee. It is used by the helper to reinforce an idea or belief previously introduced by the helpee. There are two types of influencing responses varying in intensity and persuasability. It is important that you gear your response to the level of the interaction between you and the helpee. For example, one can influence by being encouraging or threatening.[1] The order of these responses is from least to greatest intensity and one should use the latter responses with some reluctance.

Example:

Helpee: I'm not sure I really can do that.
Helper: (Encouraging)   Why don't you try; I think you can do it.
        (Threatening)   Unless you try it, we'll have to terminate the relationship.

2. Advice Giving

This response is an attempt to provide an alternative mode of action for the helpee. In general, advice giving communicates to the helpee that you have an idea that might be helpful in overcoming his problem. Often, advice giving is accompanied by the use of persuasion; i.e. "If you try this, I believe it will probably be helpful." Again, advice giving should not replace listening.

---

[1]These two are not considered separate categories since they seek the same goal and differ basically in intensity.

Example:

Helpee: I can't seem to get my work done.
Helper: Why don't you try to keep a schedule. Perhaps this will help you budget your time more effectively.

3. Questioning

In a sense all of the previous continuing and leading responses may be put in question form; i.e. "Are you saying . . . ?" However, there are times when you want to gather more information about a certain topic, focus on a particular area, or get the helpee to consider a point. Questioning is then useful. The most important consideration in asking a question is to make sure it is open-ended. A question should not be an interrogation or lead the helpee to make a yes—no response.

Helpee: John didn't call me yesterday.
Helper: (inappropriate)   Did you feel angry or hurt about not being called?
        (appropriate)   How did you feel about not being called?

In other words, questions should elicit information and feelings, not inhibit them.

ATTAINMENT LEVEL

1. Be able to identify the different leading responses.
2. Be able to use the different leading responses.

PROCEDURE

1. As a group, discuss the definitions and uses of leading responses.
2. As a group, listen to a series of helper-helpee interactions, either live or recorded, and identify the helper's leading responses.
3. In triads, listen to a series of helpee statements. You'll be asked to write down different leading responses to the statements. With the assistance of the other members of the triad, each "helper" will determine whether he was able to make effective leading responses.
4. Meet in triads and use different leading responses in a modified role playing situation. One individual should take the role of the "helper," a second the "helpee," and the third the observer. Following the modified role playing situation, the observer and "helpee" should provide feedback about the "helper's" leading responses. Each member of the triad should play each role. On page 41, there are a series of helpee-simulated statements that may be used if the triad desires.
5. Homework:
    a. Reread the definitions of the different leading responses so that you are clear on the distinctions.

b. Practice using the various leading responses with another group member. Use the modified role playing statements as a guide if necessary.

c. Respond, in writing, to several modified role playing statements by using the various leading responses (to be handed in). Respond to statements 15-20 using influencing, questioning, and advice-giving responses (see page 41).

d. Practice the responses in your daily interactions with others. Which type of response do you use most often?

e. Read Stage IV for the next session.

EVALUATION OF ATTAINMENT LEVEL

Two evaluation procedures will be used:

1. Listen to models and identify their various leading responses. You should be able to identify correctly the majority of the responses. If you are not able to identify correctly the leading responses, you will not be able to use them effectively.

2. In triads, each individual will be asked to respond to another by using all the leading responses in a modified role playing situation. *Behavioral Checklist III—Part B* is to be used as a guideline. One member of the triad should take the role of "helper," the second the "helpee," and the third the observer. Each individual should have an opportunity to play each role. Feedback will be provided by the observer and "helpee" on the "helper's" facility with the different leading responses. The feedback will serve as one source of evaluation. Your own subjective assessment will serve as a second source. If the two sources are fairly consistent, the evaluation is likely to be accurate. If there is significant discrepancy between your self evaluation and the evaluation of the observer and "helpee," attempt the evaluation again with another observer and "helpee." The trainer will be willing to act as the observer.

If your evaluation indicates a high level of leading verbal response behavior, you can feel comfortable progressing to the next stage. However, it is essential that you continually practice these responses so that they become an integral part of your interactions with others. If your evaluation indicates a less than high level, you should first identify the responses you need to improve upon and then practice them with another group member. Working with someone who exhibits à good facility with the responses you need to practice might be helpful as he will provide you with a good model.

BEHAVIORAL CHECKLIST III (PART B)
LEADING RESPONSE BEHAVIOR

	Yes	No
A. Are you able to identify correctly the following responses?		
1. Influencing	——	——
2. Advice-giving	——	——
3. Questioning	——	——

	Observer's Evaluation		"Helpee's Evaluation		Your Own Evaluation	
	Yes	No	Yes	No	Yes	No
B. Are you able to use accurately the following responses?						
1. Influencing	——	——	——	——	——	——
2. Advice-giving	——	——	——	——	——	——
3. Questioning	——	——	——	——	——	——
C. Have you achieved a sufficiently high level of skill to progress to Stage IV?	——	——	——	——	——	——

Stage III

EVALUATION OF ATTAINMENT LEVEL REPORT

NAME _____

PARTNER _____

A. The following questions pertain to your behavior during the evaluation of attainment level exercise to be done at the beginning of Stage IV. They should be completed immediately following the evaluation.

  1. From your perception, what aspects of your verbal response behavior are of poor quality?

TO BE HANDED I

2. From the perceptions of the observer and receiver, what aspects of your verbal response behavior are of poor quality?

3. Describe specifically your plans for improving your ineffective verbal response behavior.

HELPEE-SIMULATED STATEMENTS

1. 17 year old boy

You know, I'm really worried about my older brother. I mean, since he got back from Nam he's like one of those bombs—the slightest jar will set off. He can blow up at almost anything. . . My mom went to wake him the other day and he jumped up and was ready to hit her before he realized where he was and who she was. He's just a bundle of nerves. Wow—and they'll probably send me to Nam when I graduate.

2. Male college student

Gee, I really need some advice. This girl and I have been going out for about three or four months now and all of a sudden I find out that she's been seeing this other guy without telling me. Boy, was I pissed when I found that out! But then when I saw her I just didn't know how to tell her that I knew. I mean, she'd probably just say "forget it" if I got mad. I just don't know what to do, 'cause I really like her.

3. Woman in her late twenties

After 6 months, he tells me he's married. I love him. I love him so much but he says he won't leave his wife. And now he gets mad and tells me he doesn't know if he wants to see me anymore when all I do is cry around him. But I love him. I've never loved anyone else and I know I can never love anyone else again. He's my whole life. If he won't love me there's nothing for me—no point to just go on suffering. Sometimes I think I can't take it another day.

4. Male college student

I can't believe it. Everything seems so much better now. This last week I've been able to concentrate on studying. I even found some of it interesting! I got an "A" on a quiz and I haven't come close to that for two quarters. I don't know exactly why but it's like I don't have to worry so much about things anymore. I can just relax and do my thing. That's really a good feeling.

5. 35 year old man

Whenever I try to tell somebody about my really deep concerns—things that I really feel deeply about—I always feel like they don't want to hear about them. If I get the slightest hint that they aren't listening, I will just change the subject rather than continue . . . and then later I get mad at myself for not saying what I wanted to.

6.   Male college student

The reason I wanted to talk to you was that I knew you had done well in that course . . . so I thought that you would be able to give me some ideas about what I should do. But you sure haven't tried very hard to help me. I don't know anymore now than I did before I asked you.

7.   21 year old man

Whenever I get with a girl I always seem to blow it. Maybe I'm too impatient but they seem to like me at first. Like this girl I met downtown. We had a couple of drinks, danced a little, talked and then I invited her out to my trailer. She said "yes" and I thought I was in. But when we got there, she shoved me off and said she just wanted to be my friend. It's always like that. Am I so physically unattractive to women? Do I do something wrong? It's driving me up the walls. I've got to get some answers somewhere.

8.   30 year old woman

I went out to a party last week and I really enjoyed it. My husband and I were both invited but he didn't want to go so I just decided I'd go by myself and it was great! That's the first time in the eight years we've been married that I've had the courage to go anywhere by myself. I was always sure I'd be miserable or afraid he'd resent being left. My God, I've missed so much all these years because of that!

9.   25 year old woman

The trouble with you is that you really don't care about anybody. You don't care who you use or whose interests you just run over. Some hell of a counselor you are. You're always late for our sessions. When I come late, I have to explain why, but no, not you. Then the minute the hour is up you push me out the door even when I'm saying something important. Here I sit spilling my guts out and all you do is look at the clock. You must think you're pretty God damn important.

10.   Male college student

I have real trouble talking with my parents. Everytime I try to tell them about what's bothering me it seems like they don't want to hear what I say. They do such stupid things, like offer to send me more money, but that's not going to help me at all. Why don't they ever want to listen to me?

11. 45 year old man

I really don't see how my kids could say that I'm inflexible. Damn, after all I've done for them. A man can only do so much. If I give in any more, I might as well not even be around. If I don't lay down the law sometimes, they'll just take advantage of me. What can a father do these days? I try, but it's not easy being a good parent. No matter how much you try, you're never appreciated. Wait 'till they become parents!

12. Male college student

Boy, what a bind! First, they tell me that I have to go to college 'cause I need an education to get a job. But now, I finally get ready to graduate after all that plowing through those silly requirements and now no one wants to hire me. Oh, yeah, there are jobs pumping gas and waiting tables, but where's that going to get me. I probably should just be a farmer or something. If I only had the money to do that.

13. Female college student

I'm scared. It looks like I'm not going to do very well with grades this quarter. I'm getting "C's"; it's not like I'm going to flunk out. But if I don't keep my average up, I'll lose my scholarship. And if I do that, my dad will be furious. He wants me to be in school but he expects me to help with the cost of the tuition by keeping my scholarship. I just don't know what to do.

14. 22 year old woman

I'm so upset. My parents called last night and they want us to move back closer to them now that we're finishing school. But I can't stand being near them; that's half the reason I got married. I told them we were thinking of moving out West and my mother cried and talked about how they were old and had only a few more years left and everyone was deserting them and how my father is too sick to travel. I feel so awful. I cried all night. But I know if I go back there, even 100 miles away, we'll be expected to visit all the time. That would drive me crazy. I feel so guilty. I don't know what to do.

15. 40 year old woman

I feel as if I don't know how to relate to him any more. It seems like every time we talk, we end up arguing. I keep hoping that things will change and that we'll be able to enjoy each other like we used to. I don't know what's wrong; it's like there's some kind of a grudge between us. We must not be meant for each other, I guess.

16. 30 year old man

God you make me mad! So far all you have done is criticize my ideas. I try to get some help, but you don't even give a damn. Well, I'm not going to take this anymore; I can't stand it. I'll find someone who cares about helping people.

17. 25 year old man

All of us agree that he treats everyone like he's better than they are. So when I finally got up enough courage to tell him off, he turned on me and I ended up feeling stupid because I couldn't think of anything to say. In the end, I apologized and left. What a mess that was.

18. 30 year old woman

I suppose I shouldn't feel this way. I mean, you're my counselor and all. But I keep thinking of you *all* the time. I'm embarrassed to tell you some of the things I've thought about. What am I supposed to do with these feelings? I can't get anything done; all I can do is think about you. Can't you do anything to help me?

19. Female college student

This guy and I decided to live together down here at school. Of course, I couldn't tell my parents. They'd just blow up and do something really dumb, like make me quit school or not send me any more money. Anyway, last week, Bob and I had this fight and he just left, took his stuff and said he wasn't coming back. Now I don't know what to do. I don't have the money to pay for the trailer alone and I can't tell my parents. I've been so down this week, I haven't even gone to any of my classes. I keep hoping that maybe he'll come back. I just don't know.

20. Male college student

Hey, guess what happened! I just got accepted to graduate school. I was really worried that I wouldn't get in. You can't get any kind of job in psychology with only a bachelor's degree but now I don't have to worry. Wow, am I excited! They even gave me an assistantship so I'll have some money coming in. Nothing better could have happened to me!

21. Male college student

Man, I just can't see the relevance of all the courses they make us take. Some old guy stands up there and wants an audience, I guess. The stuff we have to read has no relevance to what's happening in the world now—to crime, the war, poverty, pollution, and all that stuff. That's where it's at. So why do we have to learn names and dates in ancient history and write of lot of stupid papers and all that crap.

22. 50 year old women

I really feel that I can't trust you. Everytime I leave I know you talk about me. Just the other day as I was walking down the hall before our appointment I heard you and some other people laughing about people who have problems like mine. I don't think that's very nice. Why should I tell you my problems so you can go and make fun of me?

23. 23 year old man

I don't see how you can help me. How can you know what it's like to be brought up black in the ghetto. Here you are, sitting fat, getting your big education. I had to quit school when I was 14. You'll have your job, sure, but nobody wants me. Shit, man, you'll never know where its at.

24. 45 year old man

I had to go into the hospital the other day for some diagnostic tests. And when I got there, they put me in this room with a black person—I mean, real black. He was recovering from some surgery. Well, you know, I really don't have anything against black people or anything, but it sort of bothered me—like especially when the nurses weren't around and I had to help him across the room to get to the bathroom. Well, I had feelings I just didn't like in myself.

25. Male college student

I don't know what's wrong with me. I keep finding myself looking at this guy. I mean, I'm no fag; but, God, I just don't know what's gotten into me! I just keep looking at him. I tell myself that I'm making a big thing out of nothing, but—I just don't know. It's like I *want* him to be around and to notice me. And when I try to avoid him, all I do is think about him. What am I gonna do?

26. 25 year old woman

I just can't seem to get along with anybody. I try so hard to do things that I think will please them, but it always seems to be the wrong thing. If it doesn't start an argument, it ends up that they won't even talk to me.

27. 35 year old man

How can I make people understand that I am a human being too. I've been crippled all of my life but I still feel and care as much as anyone else. Why do they treat me as if my feelings were just as insensitive as my legs?

28. Female high school student

I've really got the "blah's". I never feel sad anymore, let alone, happy. It's like everything goes in and comes out ... without any feelings at all.

29. Male high school student

I just can't seem to communicate with my parents. We must live in two completely different worlds now because whenever I try to explain to them how I feel about things, they get all upset and call me a communist.

30. 28 year old man

I really don't know if I should have come here today. I really don't think that I need a shrink or anything. Sure, I get depressed sometimes, but then, who doesn't? Well, anyway, now that I'm here, what do you want to talk about. I suppose you want to know all about my childhood and my parents and all that sort of thing, huh?

STAGE IV. USING EFFECTIVE SELF INVOLVING BEHAVIOR

GOAL

To exhibit effective self involving behavior.

RATIONALE

The rationale section for Stage II and III stressed the need for appearing competent and skillful. It was noted that helpees respond better to helpers who know what they are doing. Research indicates that in addition to "expertness," another important skill which facilitates a helping relationship is the helper's own interpersonal functioning, i.e., his ability to be a human and to convey this to the helpee. One way to convey this humanness is to allow someone to get to know you and to involve yourself in a meaningful interaction with him. There are indications that helpees are willing to let you know them in direct proportion to your willingness to let them know you. In other words, your effective self involvement becomes a model and impetus for the helpee to relate to you (and others) in a personal way.

DEFINITION

Effective self involving behavior is a two part process. First, the effective self involver responds with his personal reactions to some stimuli (behavior, attitudes, verbalization) expressed by the helpee. These reactions usually take the form of communicating the following: "I feel (this way) about (you, what you've said, what you've done)."

Some examples of these responses are:

"You know I really like you."
"That gets me angry too."
"When you do that, I guess I'm not sure whether you want to change or not."
"When you say things like that, I feel rejected."

As you will note, these responses are expressions of the *helper's* feelings.

The second part of effective self involving behavior entails expressing the reason(s) for the helper's feelings ("I feel (this way) because . . ."). These reasons often relate to the personal experiences or past histories of the helper.

47

Some examples corresponding to the responses of the first part are:

"You know I really like you. I admire people who can speak their mind."

"That gets me angry too. I need to feel that people will at least listen to what I have to say before they dismiss my ideas or feelings."

"When you do that, I guess I'm not sure whether you want to change or not. It's hard for me to believe you really want to stop drinking when you spend so much time in the bars."

"When you say things like that, I feel rejected. I have feelings too. Just because I'm supposed to be helping people doesn't mean I don't want them to like me; I do.

It is important, however, to put these behaviors in proper perspective. It is not suggested that the helper engage in mutual revelation and discussion of problems with the helpee. However, it is appropriate and facilitating to respond to the problems and feelings of others with your feelings and reactions. For example, an inappropriate self involving response might be:

Helpee: I'm having a problem with my parents and don't know what to do.
Helper: Yes, I know what you mean. My mother called me about whether I have a job for the summer. She constantly nags me too.

An appropriate self involving response:

Helpee: I'm really overwhelmed this week with work—it really gets me down.
Helper: Yes, I know how that feels. I'm trying to write a speech that's hard for me and at times I feel like forgetting the whole thing. One way I have dealt with this pressure is to . . .

GUIDELINES FOR EFFECTIVE SELF INVOLVING RESPONSES

1. Self involving statements are usually *feeling* statements rather than *belief* or *thought* statements. *Feelings* refer to emotions (warm inside, hostile, loving, blue, angry, confused, rejected, happy). Sometimes beliefs or thoughts may sound like feelings, "I feel that we will win the game," so be aware of how the word "feeling" is used.

2. Self involving statements are *direct* reports of feelings and emotions as opposed to *indirect* reports. Direct statements are personalized and active (I feel, I care, I want). Indirect statements are descriptive and passive (some people feel, "We" were talking about you and "we" decided . . .). When you use indirect statements, it is as if they don't belong to you and you are trying to attribute them to some third person. When you talk directly, you simultaneously experience and communicate your feelings and emotions.

3. Self involving statements are concerned *with* feelings and emotions, not intellectualizations *about* feelings and emotions. For example, a self involving statement concerned *about* feelings might sound like: "I have some negative feelings about talk-

ing about myself". A self involving statement concerned *with* feelings might sound like: "I don't want to talk about myself".

4. Self involving statements focus on *present* feelings and emotions rather than *past* feelings and emotions. References to *past* feelings sound like: "I always get angry at you when you're late". References to *present* feelings sound like: "I'm angry at you for being late".

ATTAINMENT LEVEL

1. To become aware of your present level of self involving behavior.
2. To increase your level of effective self involving behavior.

To understand and increase your level of self involving behavior through practice enables you as a helper to become more aware of yourself and your role in the helping relationship. As noted in Stage I, who you are and what you feel and believe influences the helping process.

PROCEDURE

1. Complete the Structured Group Interaction—Form B.H.S. Questionnaire on page 50. Following the completion of the questionnaire, you should be aware of your present level of self involving behavior.

2. Discuss as a group the implications of your level of self involving behavior and its effect on the helping relationship.

3. In dyads choose an item which neither of you have previously discussed and interact about that item with each other. The interaction should be a mutual discussion of each person's feelings about the item. Use the *Guidelines* to examine the effectiveness of your self involving behavior.

4. Observe models, either live or on film, whose discussion of an item from the S.G.I. uses a low skill level of self involving behavior.

5. In the same dyads repeat step 3 using the same S.G.I. item with a low skill level of self involving behavior.

6. Observe models discussing the same item from the S.G.I. using a high skill level of self involving behavior. Be aware of the two parts (reactions and reasons) of the self involving process as demonstrated by the models.

7. Repeat step 3 with the same partner. Use the same item with a high skill level. What were the differences between step 3 and step 7, if any?

8. Homework:
   a. Discuss an item from the S.G.I. questionnaire with a non-group member.
   b. Observe the self involving behavior of others during the week.
   c. Practice self involving behavior in your interactions during the week.
   d. To be written and handed in:

1) Think about what people you have shared personal information and feelings with (like those on the S.G.I.—B.H.S.). What is it about these people that enabled you to become involved with them? What specific characteristics do they possess?

2) Think about other people you know. Which of these would you be willing to share your feelings with and which of them wouldn't you be willing to? What specific characteristics of the people lead you to make this decision?

3) Can any generalizations be made about the characteristics of people that lead you and perhaps others to become involved personally with them? What are they?

e. Read Stage V for the next session.

f. Complete questions 1 and 2 of Part A, page 57 before the next session.

STRUCTURED GROUP INTERACTION—FORM B.H.S.

The focus of this questionnaire is to assess your feelings and perceptions about yourself as well as your willingness to involve yourself personally with others.

On the next page there are a number of statements. An understanding of your perceptions and feelings about yourself through these statements will help you become a more effective helper. Furthermore, assessing your past history of self involvement as well as your present willingness will give you information on your self involving abilities.

Therefore, in response to each statement on the next page do as follows:

1. In Column A, indicate your past self involving behavior. Enter a number in each space to indicate your previous behavior.

Enter a **1** if you have **not** discussed the item

Enter a **2** if you have discussed the item **somewhat**

Enter a **3** if you have discussed the item a **moderate amount**

Enter a **4** if you have discussed the item **fully**

For example, for question 5—"My perception of my personality"—if you have said nothing to others about this item you would put a 1 in Column A.

2. In Column B indicate your willingness to discuss the information contained in the twelve statements with another group member. Enter a number in each space to indicate your willingness to discuss each item.

Enter a **1** if you are **not** willing to discuss the item

Enter a **2** if you are **somewhat** willing to discuss the item

Enter a **3** if you are **moderately** willing to discuss the item

Enter a **4** if you are **fully** willing to discuss the item

STRUCTURED GROUP INTERACTION—FORM B.H.S.

NAME _____

	A *Past Self Involving Behavior*	B *Your Willingness to Discuss*
1. My feelings about trusting another person with information about myself		
2. The influence of my home background and parents on my perceptions of myself		
3. My perceptions of my physical appearance		
4. My perceptions of my physical appearance as compared to others' perceptions of my physical appearance		
5. My perceptions of my personality		
6. My perceptions of my personality as compared to others' perceptions of my personality		
7. My perceptions of my intellect		
8. My perceptions of my intellect as compared to others' perceptions of my intellect		
9. How important I feel my physical appearance, personality and intellect are to my feelings about myself		
10. Whether I compensate for my actual or perceived unattractive or inadequate appearance, personality or intellect and if so, how?		

	A *Past Self* *Involving Behavior*	B *Your Willingness* *to Discuss*
11. Whether my perceptions of my physical appearance, personality or intellect inhibit my interactions with others and if so, how?		
12. How much I like myself		
Sum Total of All Scores		
Average Score		

EVALUATION OF ATTAINMENT LEVEL

At the next session new dyads will be formed and step 7 will be repeated with the inclusion of a *Behavioral Checklist*. The self involving behavior should follow the *Guidelines;* namely, *direct* expressions of *present feelings* and emotions. The feedback provided by your partner on the *Behavioral Checklist* will serve as one source of evaluation. Your own subjective feelings about the effectiveness of your self involving behavior and your degree of comfort in discussing the items should also be a key in evaluating your attainment level. If the two sources are fairly consistent, the evaluation is likely to be accurate. If there is significant discrepancy between your self evaluation and the evaluation of your partner, attempt the evaluation again with another partner. The trainer will be willing to act as the observer.

If your evaluation indicated a high level of skill you can feel comfortable progressing to Stage V. Prior to Stage V you should review the first four stages since they represent the basic elements. Starting with the next stage you will be asked to apply the skills you've learned in listening accurately to another.

QUESTIONS FOR THOUGHT

The following are some questions for you to consider:

1. Do you feel as if your needs are sufficiently strong that you are able to commit yourself to being a helper? If so, why?

2. Do you feel that your needs can be fulfilled by helping others? If so, why?

3. Have your answers or feelings about the first two questions changed during the last few weeks? If so, how and why?

4. Do you feel that your past level of self involving behavior (page 52) and your willingness to self involve level (page 52) are high enough for you to be an effective helper? (Indications are that to be an adequate helper, one should be functioning at least at the 2.5 level). If you don't feel that your average levels are high enough, outline specific plans for increasing these skills. Consult the trainer if you need help.

BEHAVIORAL CHECKLIST IV
SELF INVOLVING BEHAVIOR

NAME _____

PARTNER _____

	Partner's Evaluation		Your Own Evaluation	
	Yes	No	Yes	No
1. Is the statement a feeling?	___	___	___	___
2. Is the statement a belief or thought?	___	___	___	___
3. Is the feeling expressed?	___	___	___	___
4. Is the feeling intellectualized?	___	___	___	___
5. Does the statement focus on present feelings?	___	___	___	___
6. Does the statement focus on past feelings?	___	___	___	___
7. Is the statement a direct report (personalized and active)?	___	___	___	___
8. Is the statement an indirect report (descriptive and passive)?	___	___	___	___
9. Have you achieved a sufficiently high level of skill to progress to Stage V?	___	___	___	___

Stage IV

EVALUATION OF ATTAINMENT LEVEL REPORT

NAME _____

PARTNER _____

A. The first two questions are based on your experiences during Stage IV. Please answer the questions prior to Stage V meeting.

    1. From your perceptions, how important do you think effective self involving behavior is in the helping relationship and why?

2. How do Stages I and IV relate to each other and to the whole process of being a helper?

B. The remaining questions refer to the evaluation of the attainment level and should be completed following the evaluation.

1. How well do you think your partner knows you in terms of the questionnaire item you discussed?

TO BE HANDED IN

2. (For your partner to complete) How well do you think you know your partner in terms of the questionnaire item you discussed?

3. What differences exist between these two perceptions and how can you reduce these differences?

4. Do you feel that you are at an adequate level of self involving behavior? If not, outline specific plans for increasing this level.

STAGE V. UNDERSTANDING OTHERS' COMMUNICATION

GOAL

To learn to listen effectively and accurately understand others' communications.

RATIONALE

The importance of being able to understand someone well cannot be overstated. The helper's ability to use some of the necessary communication tools is of no value if he cannot understand and listen effectively to another. Therefore, it is essential that the helper listen, observe, and feel what the other person is communicating. Understanding is more than hearing the words spoken and nodding in agreement. It is listening to the words, hearing how they are spoken, and knowing who is speaking them.

LEARNING HOW TO EFFECTIVELY UNDERSTAND OTHERS' COMMUNICATION

1. Good understanding involves:
   a. Observing (what one does)
   b. Hearing (what one says and how one says it)
   c. Feeling (how one feels)
   d. Sensing (what one has not said but wishes to)
2. Characteristics of good understanding
   a. During the previous stages, the purpose has been to acquaint you with some of the major aspects of communication: non-verbal behavior, various types of verbal responses, verbal quality and self involving behavior. The first step in good understanding is to be aware of these aspects of communication in others. For example, what and how do others communicate non-verbally; what type of verbal responses do they tend to use—questions, threats, suggestions, affective responses, self involving statements, etc. and what is their verbal quality?
   b. A second characteristic is to be aware of and make use of the first impressions you have of others. Often times, individuals say that they don't like to make judgements based on first impressions. Such a statement is comparable to closing one eye when you want to see your best or playing a game with one

arm tied behind your back. Being aware of "how one comes across initially" helps you understand something about another person and it should not be ignored. However, it is important to note that the impression one makes is not irreversible and is, in fact, tentative in that it can be changed as additional information becomes available which contradicts the original perception.

c. A third characteristic of good understanding is to avoid imposing your situation, behavior, and feelings on those of the individual to whom you are listening. When you do not distinguish between your situation and his, you are not listening effectively. Effective understanding recognizes the differences as well as similarities between people.

d. A final characteristic of good understanding is to assume nothing. In other words, distinguish between what a person says about what he does (what has happened) and what he does do (what really happened). It is not being suggested that you not trust the individual but that you be aware that discrepancies may exist between perceptions of reality and reality itself. The listener should focus on reality. The range of discrepancy is important to be aware of. For example, although an individual tells you he is happy, you should observe his behavior to see if it coincides with what he says and how he acts.

THE PROCESS OF UNDERSTANDING

In the previous section some general characteristics of accurate understanding were presented. In this section a *Model of Effective Understanding* is presented. While there are other methods of learning how to understand effectively, many individuals have found this approach useful. It requires some concentrated effort initially, but like all skills, once you practice and get familiar with this method, it will become more comfortable and automatic. An *Understanding Guide* is included to help you.

MODEL OF EFFECTIVE UNDERSTANDING

1. Within the *Understanding Guide* is a *Behavioral Index (Part A)* which lists a number of behaviors divided into several categories. As you try to understand others, be aware of their various behaviors and rate the behaviors using the words in parenthesis as a guide.

2. At the completion of the *Behavioral Index*, you should be aware of a number of behaviors others use. The process of understanding another individual involves taking all the behaviors you have noted and organizing them in a meaningful way. More than likely, you will need to discard some of the data. You should try to get some overall picture of the other person and what he is communicating. Say to yourself, "What is my best guess about this person and what he is communicating?" Remember that this picture is not final and that it is open to change as you get additional infor-

nation. It is, at present, a "best guess." To help organize the information, twenty Descriptive Organizers (Part B) are presented as part of the Understanding Guide. Using the Behavioral Index as an informational source, check as many Descriptive Organizers as are necessary to enable you to get an accurate picture of the other person. Remember this is a "best guess" and does not represent a final judgement!

3. When you have identified the Descriptive Organizers, you need to do some Impression Testing (Part C). Ask yourself the following questions:

    a. "Verbally, what is this individual saying to me?"

    b. "Behaviorally, what is this individual communicating to me?"

    c. "If a differs from b, why?"

For example, an individual may say he likes you but turn away from you, not look at you, and not respond to what you say. Therefore, a differs from b. Why? Perhaps he is trying to get you to do something for him. Perhaps he is very shy. You must look at additional behaviors to determine which one is accurate.

Remember, understanding another person is an ongoing process. These three steps therefore must be continually repeated as new behaviors or information becomes available!

ATTAINMENT LEVEL

1. To become aware of the various behaviors noted in the Behavioral Index, i.e., non-verbal behavior, type of verbal response, voice quality, etc., which individuals use in communicating.

2. To learn to translate these behaviors into a list of short-hand descriptors as noted in the Descriptive Organizers.

3. To identify your feelings and reactions toward the individual as a result of your completing the Impression Testing section.

65

UNDERSTANDING GUIDE
BEHAVIORAL INDEX—PART A

A. General Movements   *Check (if observed)*

1. Manner of walking (smooth, jerky)   _____
2. Handshake (firm, clammy, weak)   _____
3. Quality of smile (tight lipped, spontaneous, smirk)   _____
4. Face and Head Movements   _____
   a. Uses affirmative head nods   _____
   b. Face rigid   _____
   c. Calm, yet expressive use of facial movements   _____
   d. Blankly staring   _____
   e. Turning eyes away when another looks at him (her)   _____
   f. Spontaneous eye movements and eye contact   _____
   g. Not looking at other when talking   _____
   h. Looks directly at other person when he (she) talks   _____
   i. Extraneous facial movements   _____
5. Hand and Arm Movements
   a. Spontaneous and fluid use of hand and arms   _____
   b. No gesturing (arms rigid)   _____
   c. Makes physical contact with other person (shakes hands, touches arm, etc.)   _____
   d. Uses hand movements for emphasis   _____
   e. Inappropriate arm and hand movements   _____
6. Body Movements
   a. Slouching   _____
   b. Relaxed posture but not slouching   _____
   c. Sitting in fixed, rigid position   _____
7. Body Orientation
   a. Body positioned toward other   _____
   b. Physically distant from person with whom talking   _____
   c. Sits close to person with whom talking   _____
   d. Not facing other with body   _____
8. Signs of nervousness (excessive smoking, sweating, wet palms, foot shaking, restless, blushing)   _____
9. Other (identify) _____   _____

B. General Appearance
1. Dress (flashy, plain, sloppy)   _____
2. Height and weight characteristics (tall, heavy, short, well-built, thin)   _____
3. Grooming (hair, nails bitten, cleanliness)   _____
4. Handicaps (bad eyes, wheelchair, hearing aid, stutter)   _____
5. Other (identify) _____   _____

	Minimum	*Moderate*	*Excessive Use*
C. General Verbal Response Pattern			
1. No Response	——	——	——
2. Content Response	——	——	——
3. Affective Response	——	——	——
4. Encouraging	——	——	——
5. Threatening	——	——	——
6. Advice Giving	——	——	——
7. Questioning	——	——	——
8. Self Involving	——	——	——
9. Other (identify)_____	——	——	——

D. General Verbal Tone
   1. Affect level (monotone, nervous laugh, warm, cold, happy, seductive, angry)   _____
   2. Voice modulation (loud, soft)   _____
   3. Voice rhythm (fast, slow, steady, choppy)   _____
   4. Word usage (jargon, formal, psychologese, casual)   _____
   5. Other (identify)   _____

UNDERSTANDING GUIDE
DESCRIPTIVE ORGANIZERS—PART B

1. Afraid   ____
2. Anxious   ____
3. Assertive   ____
4. Caring   ____
5. Conceited   ____
6. Curious   ____
7. Defensive   ____
8. Friendly   ____
9. Hostile   ____
10. Hurt   ____
11. Impulsive   ____
12. Manipulative   ____
13. Open-minded   ____
14. Optimistic   ____
15. Passive   ____
16. Pessimistic   ____
17. Rejecting   ____
18. Reserved   ____
19. Secure   ____
20. Sensitive   ____
21. Others (identify)   ____

_____   ____

_____   ____

_____   ____

UNDERSTANDING GUIDE
IMPRESSION TESTING—PART C

1. What is the individual saying to you? _____

   _____

   _____

2. In what manner is he saying it? _____

   _____

   _____

3. What does his non-verbal behavior communicate to you? _____

   _____

4. How congruent is what the individual is saying, the manner in which he says it and his non-verbal behavior with each other?

   _____

   If not, how are they incongruent? _____

   _____

5. How do you think the degree of congruency of the factors in the above effects your Descriptive Organizer for the individual? Are your Descriptive Organizers accurate?

   _____

   _____

   Do you wish to add or delete any Descriptive Organizers? _____

   _____

6. Considering the degree of congruency for Question #4 and *then* the Descriptive Organizers you have chosen, what are your current impressions of the individual?

   _____

   _____

PROCEDURE

1. Each group member should prepare two different roles using the *Descriptive Organizers* as a guide. Be prepared to act out a 5-minute description of one of your roles during the session.

2. Review and discuss as a group the complete *Model of Effective Understanding.*

3. Observe some actors either live or on film. You will be asked to identify what their behavior communicated using the *Model of Effective Understanding.*

4. As a group discuss your perceptions of the actors as you noted from the *Model of Effective Understanding.*

5. Meet in small groups (4-6). Each group member should play one of the roles described in Step 1 and the other group members should apply and practice the *Model of Effective Understanding.*

6. Homework: (to be handed in)

    a. Practice and use the *Model of Effective Understanding* with 5 individuals. One of these individuals should be someone you don't know well and another should be someone you don't like.

    b. Read Stage VI for next week.

EVALUATION OF ATTAINMENT LEVEL

At the next session a new actor either live or on film will be introduced.

1. Complete the *Behavioral Index* for the actor. Meet in small groups (4-6) and reach a consensus about your perceptions. Individual accuracy will be determined by comparing your results with the group consensus. If your perceptions compare favorably with the group consensus, you can feel comfortable moving ahead. If your perceptions do not compare favorably, you should practice the process with group members, friends or the trainer until you can reach an effective level. The Evaluation of Attainment Level Report should be helpful in assisting you to identify your strengths and weaknesses in perceiving others' behavior.

2. Individually, complete the *Descriptive Organizers and Impression Testing* sections. Meet in the small group (4-6) and compare your understandings of the actor. Focus on the differences which exist between the perceptions of the group members.

3. At this point in the past, you have compared your progress with others to determine your attainment level. But in this stage, there will be no such comparison. The way in which you perceive and make impressions about another person is a very individual process. It is the result of your own unique history and experiences. Therefore, the important evaluation here is: (1) that you are able to use the *Model of Effective Understanding* efficiently, and (2) that you are able to determine how and why you made the impressions and reactions you did. For example, a person who had an experience of being rejected by a dark-haired woman may perceive other women with dark hair as being rejecting and feel hostile towards them.

To be an effective helper, it is necessary that you be able to recognize what it is about you that leads to the impressions you make of another person. As was stated in Stages I and IV, who you are and what you believe influences the helping process.

QUESTIONS FOR THOUGHT

Here are some questions for you to consider as you complete the evaluation:

1. Do you tend to categorize people (use the same *Descriptive Organizers* for most people)?

2. Do you tend to have similar reactions or feelings toward most people (i.e. hostility, trust, no reaction).

Stage V

EVALUATION OF ATTAINMENT LEVEL REPORT

	Yes	No
A. Are you able to effectively perceive		
1. Manner of walking	___	___
2. Handshake	___	___
3. Quality of smile	___	___
4. Face and Head Movements	___	___
5. Hand and Arm Movements	___	___
6. Body Movements	___	___
7. Body Orientation	___	___
8. Signs of nervousness	___	___
9. Other (identify) _____	___	___

B. Are you able to translate the behaviors from the *Behavioral Index* into *Descriptive Organizers*? Yes ___ No ___? If not, with what *Descriptive Organizers* do you have difficulty?

C. Are you able to make impressions about people from the *Descriptive Organizers*? Yes ___ No ___?

TO BE HANDED IN

D. Do you feel you understand and are comfortable using the complete *Model of Effective Understanding*? Yes ____ No ____? If not, what specific plans do you have to improve your understanding and use?

E. Have you achieved a sufficiently high level of skill to progress to Stage VI? Yes ____ No ____?

STAGE VI. ESTABLISHING EFFECTIVE HELPING RELATIONSHIPS

GOAL

To learn to establish effective helping relationships.

RATIONALE

During the previous stages, especially the first four, the focus of training has been on learning specific skills which facilitate the helping relationship. The focus now is on the integration of the specific skills so they can be applied in an interaction with another person, in other words, to use what you know about your helping needs in combination with effective non-verbal attending behavior, verbal response behavior, verbal tone, self involving behavior and your skill of understanding others in order to interact in a helpful manner with another. This will involve some review and practice as well as an ability to "let yourself go," i.e., to let yourself try things out without getting so anxious and nervous about doing everything just "right" that you can't be *You*. Remember, *"You"* (your personality, potential, caring, etc.) is still the best thing you have going in an interaction with another and all that has been learned during the past sessions enhances what you already were. If you get overconcerned about doing things "right," you are likely to hinder your effectiveness. Therefore, try to integrate what you've learned into your basic style of interacting. There are neither "right" ways nor mistakes: each of us does things a little differently using a basic series of skills. The only mistake you can really make is to do nothing for fear of making a mistake.

CHARACTERISTICS OF HELPING INTERACTIONS

During the initial period of interaction with another individual, attention should be focused on two skills: understanding and communicating that understanding to another person. In other words, passive understanding is insufficient: you must let the other person know that you are with him and that you understand what he is saying and *feeling*. This is communicated both verbally (see Stage III) and non-verbally (see Stage II).

There are a number of ways a person might verbally communicate with another:

75

1. By asking closed-ended and abstract questions.
   a. What school do you go to?
   b. In terms of the problem with your neighbor, have you ever thought about how many other people can't get along with a neighbor in the world.
2. By criticizing him.
   a. I would think you'd know better.
   b. That's a childish thing to do.
3. By dismissing the problem or feelings of the other person.
   a. I wouldn't worry about that; a lot of people feel that way.
   b. I don't feel that's too important.
4. By offering immediate and pat solutions.
   a. If you're not doing well, just study harder.
   b. If you are having problems with her, tell her about it.
5. By focusing your responses on the feelings and problems of the other person. (Content and Affective Responses)
   a. Are you saying (feeling) . . .
   b. Do I understand that you mean (feel) . . .
   c. It sounds like you are saying (feeling) . . .
6. By conveying your understanding and acceptance of the other person's feelings and concerns.
   a. I understand how you feel.
   b. I feel as if I know what you're saying (feeling).
7. By expressing your own feelings or relating personal experiences relevant to the other person's concerns.
   a. I can understand you're hurt; I would feel the same way.
   b. What you're saying makes me feel (happy, sad, angry, defensive, etc.).

While the first four types of responses are often used in day-to-day conversations, the latter three are more effective in helping situations. It may be easier and tempting to ask closed-ended or abstract questions, be critical, explain the problem away or offer pat and simple solutions, but resist. Instead, emphasize responding to one's feelings and conveying your understanding of them as well as sharing your own feelings with him. Furthermore, don't talk just to talk; focus on responding to him. In sum, communicate your "withness" to the other person both verbally and non-verbally. Remember your verbal responses need not be parrot or robot like. Say them naturally, but get it across!

ATTAINMENT LEVEL

1. To use effective non-verbal behavior in establishing helping relationships.
2. To be able to interact with another in a manner which verbally communicates an understanding of the other person's concerns.
3. To interact with another in a helpful manner.

PROCEDURE

1. As a group discuss the implications and processes of establishing effective helping relationships.

2. Interact in dyads with one individual being the helper and the other the helpee. The topic of communication should be a real concern the helpee has or one of the list of self involving items (Stage IV). In any case, the interaction should focus on real feelings and events not role playing. Each member of the dyad should have an opportunity to be both the helper and helpee.

3. Observe models, either live or on film, using ineffective communication skills.

4. Repeat Step 2 using ineffective communication skills.

5. Observe models using effective communication skills.

6. Repeat Step 2 using effective communication skills.

7. As a group discuss the difference in behavior when poor and good communication skills are used.

8. Homework:

a. Meet with a different group member and repeat Step 6. Each individual should have an opportunity to be the helper for about 20 minutes. If possible, audiotape the session and before switching roles listen to the tape and evaluate the effectiveness of the communication skills being used. The Checklist on page 79 can serve as a guide.

b. Observe the communication skills of others. Do they use effective skills? If not, why?

c. In interacting with others this week, concentrate on avoiding casual or ineffective helping responses. Focus on understanding and communicating your understanding to others. As in other skills it may be awkward at first; however, work hard at it. What kind of response do you get from others when you respond this way; is it different than usual?

d. (to be handed in) Meet with a non-group member whom you do not know very well. In your interaction with him, use the *Model of Effective Understanding* together with your perceptions about him. As you are developing your perceptions, try to establish an effective helping relationship.

Following the interaction, complete a sample *Behavioral Checklist* both as you rate yourself and as if you were the other person rating you. In addition, answer the following question about your interaction:

(1) Are your perceptions of him based on the way you perceive people-in-general (categorizing) or are they specifically directed to your immediate perceptions of him. Explain the reasons for your choice.

(2) Overall, how would you characterize the effectiveness of your relationship?

EVALUATION OF ATTAINMENT LEVEL

At the next session triads will be formed and Step #5 will be repeated with one member of the triad serving as the helper, a second serving as the helpee and the third as the observer. Each member of the triad should have an opportunity to be a helper, a helpee, and an observer. In order to help evaluate your progress a *Behavioral Checklist* is included. The feedback provided by the helpee and the observer will serve as one source of evaluation. Your own subjective assessment will serve as a second source. If the two sources are fairly consistent, the evaluation is likely to be accurate. If there is a significant discrepancy between your self evaluation and the evaluation of the observer and the helpee, attempt the evaluation again with another helpee and observer. The trainer will be willing to act as the observer.

If your evaluation indicates a high level of skill, you can feel comfortable progressing to the next activity. If your evaluation indicates less than a high level of skill at establishing relationships, you should first identify the areas you need to improve and practice with another group member. Working with someone who has effective communication skills might be helpful since it will provide you with a good model.

BEHAVIORAL CHECKLIST VI.
ESTABLISHING EFFECTIVE HELPING RELATIONSHIPS

HELPER _____

HELPEE _____

OBSERVER _____

	Observer and Helpee Feedback		Your Own Evaluation	
	Yes	No	Yes	No
1. Did the helper ask a lot of close-ended questions?	——	——	——	——
2. Did the helper ask a lot of abstract questions?	——	——	——	——
3. Did the helper tend to ask too many questions?	——	——	——	——
4. Did the helper tend to criticize the helpee for his actions?	——	——	——	——
5. Did the helper tend to interrupt the helpee?	——	——		
6. Did the helper tend to dismiss the problems or feelings of the helpee?	——	——	——	——
7. Did the helper tend to offer pat or immediate solutions for the helpee's concerns?	——	——	——	——
8. Did the helper focus his (her) responses on the feelings and problems of the helpee?	——	——	——	——
9. Did the helper convey understanding and acceptance of the helpee's feelings and concerns?	——	——	——	——
10. Did the helper present himself more as an authority figure than as an equal?	——	——	——	——
11. Did the helper express any of his (her) own feelings or personal experiences relevant to the helpee's concerns?	——	——	——	——
12. Did the helper tend to avoid direct questions and concerns presented to him by the helpee?	——	——	——	——

NOT TO BE HANDED IN

13. In general, how effective was the helper in communicating understanding to the helpee?

       Excellent ___
       Good   ___
       Fair   ___
       Poor   ___

14. Have you achieved a sufficiently high level of skill on this stage?

    ___ ___   ___ ___

Stage VI

EVALUATION OF ATTAINMENT LEVEL REPORT

NAME_____

PARTNER_____

A. Answer the following questions during the evaluation of attainment level exercise to be done at the beginning of the final session. These should be completed immediately following the evaluation.

1. How effective are you at establishing effective helping relationships? Why?

2. From the perceptions of the observer and helpee, how effective are you at establishing effective helping relationships? Why?

3. Describe specifically your plans for improving your effectiveness at establishing helping relationships?

Appendix:
Additional Behavioral Checklists for Homework

BEHAVIOR CHECKLIST II
NON-VERBAL BEHAVIOR FOR HOMEWORK

Behavior Observed (Check if observed)

	Discussant I	*Discussant II*
A. Face and Head Movements		
1. Uses affirmative head nods	——	——
2. Face rigid	——	——
3. Calm, yet expressive use of facial movements	——	——
4. Blankly staring	——	——
5. Turning eyes away when another looks at him (her)	——	——
6. Spontaneous eye movements and eye contact	——	——
7. Not looking at other when talking	——	——
8. Looks directly at other person when he (she) talks	——	——
9. Extraneous facial movements	——	——
B. Hand and Arm Movements		
10. Spontaneous and fluid use of hand and arms	——	——
11. No gesturing (arms rigid)	——	——
12. Makes physical contact with other person (shakes hands, touches arm, etc.)	——	——
13. Uses hand movements for emphasis	——	——
14. Inappropriate arm and hand movements	——	——
C. Body Movements		
15. Slouching	——	——
16. Relaxed posture but not slouching	——	——
17. Sitting in fixed, rigid position	——	——
D. Body Orientation		
18. Body positioned toward other	——	——
19. Physically distant from person	——	——
20. Sits close to person with whom talking	——	——
21. Not facing other with body	——	——

E. Verbal Quality   *Discussant I*   *Discussant II*
    22. Voice quiver   ____   ____
    23. Speech blocks or stammers   ____   ____
    24. Lack of affect   ____   ____
    25. Inappropriate affect   ____   ____
    26. Too loud   ____   ____
    27. Too soft   ____   ____
    28. Excessive use of jargon   ____   ____
    29. Excessive use of "psychologese"   ____   ____
    30. Excessive use of "you know"   ____   ____
    31. Too fast   ____   ____
    32. Too slow   ____   ____

F. Have you achieved a sufficiently high level
    of skill to progress to Stage III?   ____   ____

BEHAVIOR CHECKLIST II
NON-VERBAL BEHAVIOR FOR HOMEWORK

Behavior Observed (Check if observed)

	Discussant I	*Discussant II*
A. Face and Head Movements		
1. Uses affirmative head nods	——	——
2. Face rigid	——	——
3. Calm, yet expressive use of facial movements	——	——
4. Blankly staring	——	——
5. Turning eyes away when another looks at him (her)	——	——
6. Spontaneous eye movements and eye contact	——	——
7. Not looking at other when talking	——	——
8. Looks directly at other person when he (she) talks	——	——
9. Extraneous facial movements	——	——
B. Hand and Arm Movements		
10. Spontaneous and fluid use of hand and arms	——	——
11. No gesturing (arms rigid)	——	——
12. Makes physical contact with other person (shakes hands, touches arm, etc.)	——	——
13. Uses hand movements for emphasis	——	——
14. Inappropriate arm and hand movements	——	——
C. Body Movements		
15. Slouching	——	——
16. Relaxed posture but not slouching	——	——
17. Sitting in fixed, rigid position	——	——
D. Body Orientation		
18. Body positioned toward other	——	——
19. Physically distant from person	——	——
20. Sits close to person with whom talking	——	——
21. Not facing other with body	——	——

TO BE HANDED IN

		Discussant I	_Discussant II_
E.	Verbal Quality		
	22. Voice quiver	___	___
	23. Speech blocks or stammers	___	___
	24. Lack of affect	___	___
	25. Inappropriate affect	___	___
	26. Too loud	___	___
	27. Too soft	___	___
	28. Excessive use of jargon	___	___
	29. Excessive use of "psychologese"	___	___
	30. Excessive use of "you know"	___	___
	31. Too fast	___	___
	32. Too slow	___	___
F.	Have you achieved a sufficiently high level of skill to progress to Stage III?	___	___

BEHAVIOR CHECKLIST II
NON-VERBAL BEHAVIOR FOR HOMEWORK

Behavior Observed (Check if observed)

	Discussant I	*Discussant II*
A. Face and Head Movements		
1. Uses affirmative head nods	——	——
2. Face rigid	——	——
3. Calm, yet expressive use of facial movements	——	——
4. Blankly staring	——	——
5. Turning eyes away when another looks at him (her)	——	——
6. Spontaneous eye movements and eye contact	——	——
7. Not looking at other when talking	——	——
8. Looks directly at other person when he (she) talks	——	——
9. Extraneous facial movements	——	——
B. Hand and Arm Movements		
10. Spontaneous and fluid use of hand and arms	——	——
11. No gesturing (arms rigid)	——	——
12. Makes physical contact with other person (shakes hands, touches arm, etc.)	——	——
13. Uses hand movements for emphasis	——	——
14. Inappropriate arm and hand movements	——	——
C. Body Movements		
15. Slouching	——	——
16. Relaxed posture but not slouching	——	——
17. Sitting in fixed, rigid position	——	——
D. Body Orientation		
18. Body positioned toward other	——	——
19. Physically distant from person	——	——
20. Sits close to person with whom talking	——	——
21. Not facing other with body	——	——

TO BE HANDED IN

		Discussant I	*Discussant II*
E.	Verbal Quality		
	22. Voice quiver	____	____
	23. Speech blocks or stammers	____	____
	24. Lack of affect	____	____
	25. Inappropriate affect	____	____
	26. Too loud	____	____
	27. Too soft	____	____
	28. Excessive use of jargon	____	____
	29. Excessive use of "psychologese"	____	____
	30. Excessive use of "you know"	____	____
	31. Too fast	____	____
	32. Too slow	____	____
F.	Have you achieved a sufficiently high level of skill to progress to Stage III?	____	____

UNDERSTANDING GUIDE
BEHAVIORAL INDEX—PART A

A. General Movements   *Check (if observed)*

1. Manner of walking (smooth, jerky)   _____
2. Handshake (firm, clammy, weak)   _____
3. Quality of smile (tight lipped, spontaneous, smirk)   _____
4. Face and Head Movements   _____
    a. Uses affirmative head nods   _____
    b. Face rigid   _____
    c. Calm, yet expressive use of facial movements   _____
    d. Blankly staring   _____
    e. Turning eyes away when another looks at him (her)   _____
    f. Spontaneous eye movements and eye contact   _____
    g. Not looking at other when talking   _____
    h. Looks directly at other person when he (she) talks   _____
    i. Extraneous facial movements   _____
5. Hand and Arm Movements
    a. Spontaneous and fluid use of hand and arms   _____
    b. No gesturing (arms rigid)   _____
    c. Makes physical contact with other person (shakes hands, touches arm, etc.)   _____
    d. Uses hand movements for emphasis   _____
    e. Inappropriate arm and hand movements   _____
6. Body Movements
    a. Slouching   _____
    b. Relaxed posture but not slouching   _____
    c. Sitting in fixed, rigid position   _____
7. Body Orientation
    a. Body positioned toward other   _____
    b. Physically distant from person with whom talking   _____
    c. Sits close to person with whom talking   _____
    d. Not facing other with body   _____
8. Signs of nervousness (excessive smoking, sweating, wet palms, foot shaking, restless, blushing)   _____
9. Other (identify) _____   _____

B. General Appearance
1. Dress (flashy, plain, sloppy)   _____
2. Height and weight characteristics (tall, heavy, short, well-built, thin)   _____
3. Grooming (hair, nails bitten, cleanliness)   _____
4. Handicaps (bad eyes, wheelchair, hearing aid, stutter)   _____
5. Other (identify) _____   _____

TO BE HANDED IN

	Minimum	Moderate	Excessive Use
C. General Verbal Response Pattern			
1. No Response	___	___	___
2. Content Response	___	___	___
3. Affective Response	___	___	___
4. Encouraging	___	___	___
5. Threatening	___	___	___
6. Advice Giving	___	___	___
7. Questioning	___	___	___
8. Self Involving	___	___	___
9. Other (identify) _____	___	___	___

D. General Verbal Tone
1. Affect level (monotone, nervous laugh, warm, cold, happy, seductive, angry) _____
2. Voice modulation (loud, soft) _____
3. Voice rhythm (fast, slow, steady, choppy) _____
4. Word usage (jargon, formal, psychologese, casual) _____
5. Other (identify) _____

UNDERSTANDING GUIDE
BEHAVIORAL INDEX—PART A

A. General Movements   *Check (if observed)*

1. Manner of walking (smooth, jerky) _____
2. Handshake (firm, clammy, weak) _____
3. Quality of smile (tight lipped, spontaneous, smirk) _____
4. Face and Head Movements _____
   a. Uses affirmative head nods _____
   b. Face rigid _____
   c. Calm, yet expressive use of facial movements _____
   d. Blankly staring _____
   e. Turning eyes away when another looks at him (her) _____
   f. Spontaneous eye movements and eye contact _____
   g. Not looking at other when talking _____
   h. Looks directly at other person when he (she) talks _____
   i. Extraneous facial movements _____
5. Hand and Arm Movements
   a. Spontaneous and fluid use of hand and arms _____
   b. No gesturing (arms rigid) _____
   c. Makes physical contact with other person (shakes hands, touches arm, etc.) _____
   d. Uses hand movements for emphasis _____
   e. Inappropriate arm and hand movements _____
6. Body Movements
   a. Slouching _____
   b. Relaxed posture but not slouching _____
   c. Sitting in fixed, rigid position _____
7. Body Orientation
   a. Body positioned toward other _____
   b. Physically distant from person with whom talking _____
   c. Sits close to person with whom talking _____
   d. Not facing other with body _____
8. Signs of nervousness (excessive smoking, sweating, wet palms, foot shaking, restless, blushing) _____
9. Other (identify)_____ _____

B. General Appearance
1. Dress (flashy, plain, sloppy) _____
2. Height and weight characteristics (tall, heavy, short, well-built, thin) _____
3. Grooming (hair, nails bitten, cleanliness) _____
4. Handicaps (bad eyes, wheelchair, hearing aid, stutter) _____
5. Other (identify)_____ _____

	Minimum	Moderate	Excessive Use
C. General Verbal Response Pattern			
1. No Response	___	___	___
2. Content Response	___	___	___
3. Affective Response	___	___	___
4. Encouraging	___	___	___
5. Threatening	___	___	___
6. Advice Giving	___	___	___
7. Questioning	___	___	___
8. Self Involving	___	___	___
9. Other (identify) _____	___	___	___

D. General Verbal Tone
  1. Affect level (monotone, nervous laugh, warm, cold, happy, seductive, angry)   _____
  2. Voice modulation (loud, soft)   _____
  3. Voice rhythm (fast, slow, steady, choppy)   _____
  4. Word usage (jargon, formal, psychologese, casual)   _____
  5. Other (identify)   _____

UNDERSTANDING GUIDE
BEHAVIORAL INDEX—PART A

Check (if observed)

A. General Movements
1. Manner of walking (smooth, jerky) _____
2. Handshake (firm, clammy, weak) _____
3. Quality of smile (tight lipped, spontaneous, smirk) _____
4. Face and Head Movements _____
   a. Uses affirmative head nods _____
   b. Face rigid _____
   c. Calm, yet expressive use of facial movements _____
   d. Blankly staring _____
   e. Turning eyes away when another looks at him (her) _____
   f. Spontaneous eye movements and eye contact _____
   g. Not looking at other when talking _____
   h. Looks directly at other person when he (she) talks _____
   i. Extraneous facial movements _____
5. Hand and Arm Movements
   a. Spontaneous and fluid use of hand and arms _____
   b. No gesturing (arms rigid) _____
   c. Makes physical contact with other person (shakes hands, touches arm, etc.) _____
   d. Uses hand movements for emphasis _____
   e. Inappropriate arm and hand movements _____
6. Body Movements
   a. Slouching _____
   b. Relaxed posture but not slouching _____
   c. Sitting in fixed, rigid position _____
7. Body Orientation
   a. Body positioned toward other _____
   b. Physically distant from person with whom talking _____
   c. Sits close to person with whom talking _____
   d. Not facing other with body _____
8. Signs of nervousness (excessive smoking, sweating, wet palms, foot shaking, restless, blushing) _____
9. Other (identify) _____ _____

B. General Appearance
1. Dress (flashy, plain, sloppy) _____
2. Height and weight characteristics (tall, heavy, short, well-built, thin) _____
3. Grooming (hair, nails bitten, cleanliness) _____
4. Handicaps (bad eyes, wheelchair, hearing aid, stutter) _____
5. Other (identify) _____ _____

TO BE HANDED IN

	Minimum	Moderate	Excessive Use
C. General Verbal Response Pattern			
1. No Response	___	___	___
2. Content Response	___	___	___
3. Affective Response	___	___	___
4. Encouraging	___	___	___
5. Threatening	___	___	___
6. Advice Giving	___	___	___
7. Questioning	___	___	___
8. Self Involving	___	___	___
9. Other (identify) _____	___	___	___

D. General Verbal Tone
1. Affect level (monotone, nervous laugh, warm, cold, happy, seductive, angry)   _____
2. Voice modulation (loud, soft)   _____
3. Voice rhythm (fast, slow, steady, choppy)   _____
4. Word usage (jargon, formal, psychologese, casual)   _____
   Other (identify)   _____

UNDERSTANDING GUIDE
BEHAVIORAL INDEX—PART A

A. General Movements   *Check (if observed)*
   1. Manner of walking (smooth, jerky)   _____
   2. Handshake (firm, clammy, weak)   _____
   3. Quality of smile (tight lipped, spontaneous, smirk)   _____
   4. Face and Head Movements   _____
     a. Uses affirmative head nods   _____
     b. Face rigid   _____
     c. Calm, yet expressive use of facial movements _____
     d. Blankly staring   _____
     e. Turning eyes away when another looks at him (her) _____
     f. Spontaneous eye movements and eye contact   _____
     g. Not looking at other when talking   _____
     h. Looks directly at other person when he (she) talks _____
     i. Extraneous facial movements   _____
   5. Hand and Arm Movements
     a. Spontaneous and fluid use of hand and arms   _____
     b. No gesturing (arms rigid)   _____
     c. Makes physical contact with other person (shakes hands, touches arm, etc.)   _____
     d. Uses hand movements for emphasis   _____
     e. Inappropriate arm and hand movements   _____
   6. Body Movements
     a. Slouching   _____
     b. Relaxed posture but not slouching   _____
     c. Sitting in fixed, rigid position   _____
   7. Body Orientation
     a. Body positioned toward other   _____
     b. Physically distant from person with whom talking _____
     c. Sits close to person with whom talking   _____
     d. Not facing other with body   _____
   8. Signs of nervousness (excessive smoking, sweating, wet palms, foot shaking, restless, blushing)   _____
   9. Other (identify) _____   _____

B. General Appearance
   1. Dress (flashy, plain, sloppy)   _____
   2. Height and weight characteristics (tall, heavy, short, well-built, thin)   _____
   3. Grooming (hair, nails bitten, cleanliness)   _____
   4. Handicaps (bad eyes, wheelchair, hearing aid, stutter) _____
   5. Other (identify) _____   _____

TO BE HANDED IN

C. General Verbal Response Pattern	Minimum	Moderate	Excessive Use
1. No Response	____	____	____
2. Content Response	____	____	____
3. Affective Response	____	____	____
4. Encouraging	____	____	____
5. Threatening	____	____	____
6. Advice Giving	____	____	____
7. Questioning	____	____	____
8. Self Involving	____	____	____
9. Other (identify) _____	____	____	____

D. General Verbal Tone
   1. Affect level (monotone, nervous laugh, warm, cold, happy, seductive, angry)   _____
   2. Voice modulation (loud, soft)   _____
   3. Voice rhythm (fast, slow, steady, choppy)   _____
   4. Word usage (jargon, formal, psychologese, casual)   _____
   5. Other (identify)   _____

UNDERSTANDING GUIDE
BEHAVIORAL INDEX—PART A

A. General Movements   *Check (if observed)*
   1. Manner of walking (smooth, jerky)   _____
   2. Handshake (firm, clammy, weak)   _____
   3. Quality of smile (tight lipped, spontaneous, smirk)   _____
   4. Face and Head Movements   _____
      a. Uses affirmative head nods   _____
      b. Face rigid   _____
      c. Calm, yet expressive use of facial movements   _____
      d. Blankly staring   _____
      e. Turning eyes away when another looks at him (her)   _____
      f. Spontaneous and fluid use of hand and arms   _____
      g. Not looking at other when talking   _____
      h. Looks directly at other person when he (she) talks   _____
      i. Extraneous facial movements   _____
   5. Hand and Arm Movements
      a. Spontaneous and fluid use of hand and arms   _____
      b. No gesturing (arms rigid)   _____
      c. Makes physical contact with other person (shakes hands,
         touches arm, etc.)   _____
      d. Uses hand movements for emphasis   _____
      e. Inappropriate arm and hand movements   _____
   6. Body Movements
      a. Slouching   _____
      b. Relaxed posture but not slouching   _____
      c. Sitting in fixed, rigid position   _____
   7. Body Orientation
      a. Body positioned toward other   _____
      b. Physically distant from person with whom talking   _____
      c. Sits close to person with whom talking   _____
      d. Not facing other with body   _____
   8. Signs of nervousness (excessive smoking, sweating, wet palms,
      foot shaking, restless, blushing)   _____
   9. Other (identify)_____   _____

B. General Appearance
   1. Dress (flashy, plain, sloppy)   _____
   2. Height and weight characteristics (tall, heavy, short, well-
      built, thin)   _____
   3. Grooming (hair, nails bitten, cleanliness)   _____
   4. Handicaps (bad eyes, wheelchair, hearing aid, stutter)   _____
   5. Other (identify)_____   _____

TO BE HANDED IN

	Minimum	moderate	Excessive Use
C. General Verbal Response Pattern			
1. No Response	____	____	____
2. Content Response	____	____	____
3. Affective Response	____	____	____
4. Encouraging	____	____	____
5. Threatening	____	____	____
6. Advice Giving	____	____	____
7. Questioning	____	____	____
8. Self Involving	____	____	____
9. Other (identify)_____	____	____	____

D. General Verbal Tone
   1. Affect level (monotone, nervous laugh, warm, cold, happy, seductive, angry)
   2. Voice modulation (loud, soft)   _____
   3. Voice rhythm (fast, slow, steady, choppy)   _____
   4. Word usage (jargon, formal, psychologese, casual)   _____
   5. Other (identify)   _____

UNDERSTANDING GUIDE
DESCRIPTIVE ORGANIZERS—PART B

1. Afraid ＿＿
2. Anxious ＿＿
3. Assertive ＿＿
4. Caring ＿＿
5. Conceited ＿＿
6. Curious ＿＿
7. Defensive ＿＿
8. Friendly ＿＿
9. Hostile ＿＿
10. Hurt ＿＿
11. Impulsive ＿＿
12. Manipulative ＿＿
13. Open-minded ＿＿
14. Optimistic ＿＿
15. Passive ＿＿
16. Pessimistic ＿＿
17. Rejecting ＿＿
18. Reserved ＿＿
19. Secure ＿＿
20. Sensitive ＿＿
21. Others (identify) ＿＿

＿＿＿＿＿＿ ＿＿
＿＿＿＿＿＿ ＿＿
＿＿＿＿＿＿ ＿＿

UNDERSTANDING GUIDE
DESCRIPTIVE ORGANIZERS—PART B

1. Afraid ——
2. Anxious ——
3. Assertive ——
4. Caring ——
5. Conceited ——
6. Curious ——
7. Defensive ——
8. Friendly ——
9. Hostile ——
10. Hurt ——
11. Impulsive ——
12. Manipulative ——
13. Open-minded ——
14. Optimistic ——
15. Passive ——
16. Pessimistic ——
17. Rejecting ——
18. Reserved ——
19. Secure ——
20. Sensitive ——
21. Others (identify) ——

_____ ——
_____ ——
_____ ——

UNDERSTANDING GUIDE
DESCRIPTIVE ORGANIZERS—PART B

1. Afraid   ————
2. Anxious   ————
3. Assertive   ————
4. Caring   ————
5. Conceited   ————
6. Curious   ————
7. Defensive   ————
8. Friendly   ————
9. Hostile   ————
10. Hurt   ————
11. Impulsive   ————
12. Manipulative   ————
13. Open-minded   ————
14. Optimistic   ————
15. Passive   ————
16. Pessimistic   ————
17. Rejecting   ————
18. Reserved   ————
19. Secure   ————
20. Sensitive   ————
21. Others (identify)   ————

_____ ————
_____ ————
_____ ————

UNDERSTANDING GUIDE
DESCRIPTIVE ORGANIZERS—PART B

1. Afraid   ——
2. Anxious   ——
3. Assertive   ——
4. Caring   ——
5. Conceited   ——
6. Curious   ——
7. Defensive   ——
8. Friendly   ——
9. Hostile   ——
10. Hurt   ——
11. Impulsive   ——
12. Manipulative   ——
13. Open-minded   ——
14. Optimistic   ——
15. Passive   ——
16. Pessimistic   ——
17. Rejecting   ——
18. Reserved   ——
19. Secure   ——
20. Sensitive   ——
21. Others (identify)   ——

   _____   ——

   _____   ——

   _____   ——

UNDERSTANDING GUIDE
DESCRIPTIVE ORGANIZERS—PART B

1. Afraid   ——
2. Anxious   ——
3. Assertive   ——
4. Caring   ——
5. Conceited   ——
6. Curious   ——
7. Defensive   ——
8. Friendly   ——
9. Hostile   ——
10. Hurt   ——
11. Impulsive   ——
12. Manipulative   ——
13. Open-minded   ——
14. Optimistic   ——
15. Passive   ——
16. Pessimistic   ——
17. Rejecting   ——
18. Reserved   ——
19. Secure   ——
20. Sensitive   ——
21. Others (identify)   ——

   _____ ——
   _____ ——
   _____ ——

UNDERSTANDING GUIDE
IMPRESSION TESTING—PART C

1. What is the individual saying to you? _____

   _____

   _____

2. In what manner is he saying it? _____

   _____

   _____

3. What does his non-verbal behavior communicate to you? _____

   _____

   _____

4. How congruent is what the individual is saying, the manner in which he says it and his non-verbal behavior with each other?

   _____

   If not, how are they incongruent? _____

   _____

5. How do you think the degree of congruency of the factors in the above effects your Descriptive Organizer for the individual? Are your Descriptive Organizers accurate?

   _____

   _____

   Do you wish to add or delete any Descriptive Organizers? _____

   _____

6. Considering the degree of congruency for Question #4 and *then* the Descriptive Organizers you have chosen, what are your current impressions of the individual?

   _____

   _____

UNDERSTANDING GUIDE
IMPRESSION TESTING—PART C

1. What is the individual saying to you? _____

_____

_____

2. In what manner is he saying it? _____

_____

_____

3. What does his non-verbal behavior communicate to you? _____

_____

_____

4. How congruent is what the individual is saying, the manner in which he says it and his non-verbal behavior with each other?

_____

If not, how are they incongruent? _____

_____

5. How do you think the degree of congruency of the factors in the above effects your Descriptive Organizer for the individual? Are your Descriptive Organizers accurate?

_____

_____

Do you wish to add or delete any Descriptive Organizers? _____

_____

6. Considering the degree of congruency for Question #4 and *then* the Descriptive Organizers you have chosen, what are your current impressions of the individual?

_____

_____

UNDERSTANDING GUIDE
IMPRESSION TESTING—PART C

1. What is the individual saying to you? _____

_____

_____

2. In what manner is he saying it? _____

_____

_____

3. What does his non-verbal behavior communicate to you? _____

_____

_____

4. How congruent is what the individual is saying, the manner in which he says it and his non-verbal behavior with each other?

_____

    If not, how are they incongruent? _____

_____

5. How do you think the degree of congruency of the factors in the above effects your Descriptive Organizer for the individual? Are your Descriptive Organizers accurate?

_____

_____

    Do you wish to add or delete any Descriptive Organizers? _____

_____

6. Considering the degree of congruency for Question #4 and *then* the Descriptive Organizers you have chosen, what are your current impressions of the individual?

_____

_____

UNDERSTANDING GUIDE
IMPRESSION TESTING—PART C

1. What is the individual saying to you? _____

_____

_____

2. In what manner is he saying it? _____

_____

_____

3. What does his non-verbal behavior communicate to you? _____

_____

_____

4. How congruent is what the individual is saying, the manner in which he says it and his non-verbal behavior with each other?

_____

If not, how are they incongruent? _____

_____

5. How do you think the degree of congruency of the factors in the above effects your Descriptive Organizer for the individual? Are your Descriptive Organizers accurate?

_____

_____

Do you wish to add or delete any Descriptive Organizers? _____

_____

6. Considering the degree of congruency for Question #4 and *then* the Descriptive Organizers you have chosen, what are your current impressions of the individual?

_____

_____

UNDERSTANDING GUIDE
IMPRESSION TESTING—PART C

1. What is the individual saying to you? _____

_____

_____

2. In what manner is he saying it? _____

_____

_____

3. What does his non-verbal behavior communicate to you? _____

_____

_____

4. How congruent is what the individual is saying, the manner in which he says it and his non-verbal behavior with each other?

_____

If not, how are they incongruent? _____

_____

5. How do you think the degree of congruency of the factors in the above effects your Descriptive Organizer for the individual? Are your Descriptive Organizers accurate?

_____

_____

Do you wish to add or delete any Descriptive Organizers? _____

_____

6. Considering the degree of congruency for Question #4 and *then* the Descriptive Organizers you have chosen, what are your current impressions of the individual?

_____

_____

121

NOT TO BE HANDED IN

BEHAVIORAL CHECKLIST VI.
ESTABLISHING EFFECTIVE HELPING RELATIONSHIPS

HELPER _____

HELPEE _____

OBSERVER _____

	Observer and Helpee Feedback		Your Own Evaluation	
	Yes	No	Yes	No
1. Did the helper ask a lot of close-ended questions?	___	___	___	___
2. Did the helper ask a lot of abstract questions?	___	___	___	___
3. Did the helper tend to ask too many questions?	___	___	___	___
4. Did the helper tend to criticize the helpee for his actions?	___	___	___	___
5. Did the helper tend to interrupt the helpee?	___	___		
6. Did the helper tend to dismiss the problems or feelings of the helpee?	___	___	___	___
7. Did the helper tend to offer pat or immediate solutions for the helpee's concerns?	___	___	___	___
8. Did the helper focus his (her) responses on the feelings and problems of the helpee?	___	___	___	___
9. Did the helper convey understanding and acceptance of the helpee's feelings and concerns?	___	___	___	___
10. Did the helper present himself more as an authority figure than as an equal?	___	___	___	___
11. Did the helper express any of his (her) own feelings or personal experiences relevant to the helpee's concerns?	___	___	___	___
12. Did the helper tend to avoid direct questions and concerns presented to him by the helpee?	___	___	___	___

NOT TO BE HANDED IN

13. In general, how effective was the helper in commu-
    nicating understanding to the helpee?

    Excellent ___
    Good   ___
    Fair   ___
    Poor   ___

14. Have you achieved a sufficiently high level of skill
    on this stage?

    ___ ___   ___ ___